Importance of Business Culture

Laurel D. Malvern

Copyright and Legal Disclaimer:

Copyright © 2024 by Laurel D. Malvern. All rights reserved.

No part of this book, "Importance of Business Culture," may be reproduced, stored in a retrieval system, or transmitted in any form or by any means, electronic, mechanical, photocopying, recording, scanning, or otherwise, without the prior written permission of the publisher, except as permitted by the Copyright Act of 1976.

This book is a work of non-fiction. The information provided herein is for educational and informational purposes only and is not intended as legal, business, or professional advice. Readers are advised to consult with appropriate professionals regarding their specific situations and needs.

The author and publisher make no representations or warranties with respect to the accuracy, applicability, completeness, or suitability of the contents of this book. They disclaim any liability arising from the use of information contained herein.

Any trademarks, service marks, product names, or company names mentioned in this book are used for identification purposes only and do not imply endorsement. Their use in this book does not imply that they are affiliated with the author or publisher.

The views expressed in this book are those of the author alone and do not necessarily reflect the views of the publisher or any organization with which the author may be affiliated.

While every effort has been made to ensure the accuracy of the information presented in this book, the author and publisher cannot be held responsible for any errors or omissions that may occur.

For permissions inquiries or other questions, please contact the publisher.

"Importance of Business Culture"

Preface: 8

Introduction: 10

Chapter 1: Setting the Stage: Defining Business Culture 11

Chapter 2: Why Business Culture Matters: Impact on Success and Sustainability 13

Chapter 3: Understanding Business Culture 15

Chapter 4: What is Business Culture? 17

Chapter 5: Elements of Business Culture 19

Chapter 6: Values and Beliefs 21

Chapter 7: Communication Styles 23

Chapter 8: Organizational Structure 25

Chapter 9: Work Environment 27

Chapter 10: Rituals and Traditions 29

Chapter 11: The Role of Business Culture in Success 31

Chapter 12: Building Trust and Engagement 34

Chapter 13: Fostering Innovation and Creativity 37

Chapter 14: Enhancing Employee Satisfaction and Retention 40

Chapter 15: Improving Collaboration and Teamwork 43

Chapter 16: Navigating Cultural Differences 46

Chapter 17: Globalization and Cultural Diversity in Business 49

Chapter 18: Challenges and Opportunities of Cross-Cultural Communication 52

Chapter 19: Strategies for Managing Cultural Differences 55

Chapter 20: Creating a Positive Business Culture 58

Chapter 21: Leadership's Role in Shaping Culture 61

Chapter 22: Establishing Core Values and Mission 64

Chapter 23: Promoting Diversity, Equity, and Inclusion 67

Chapter 24: Cultivating a Growth Mindset 70

Chapter 25: Encouraging Work-Life Balance 73

Chapter 26: Case Studies: Exemplary Business Cultures 76

Chapter 27: Companies That Have Successfully Nurtured a Positive Culture 79

Chapter 28: Lessons Learned from Their Journeys 82

Chapter 29: Assessing and Improving Your Business Culture 85

Chapter 30: Tools and Methods for Assessing Organizational Culture 88

Chapter 31: Identifying Areas for Improvement 92

Chapter 32: Implementing Changes and Measuring Impact 95

Chapter 33: The Future of Business Culture 98

Chapter 34: Trends Shaping the Future of Work and Culture 101

Chapter 35: Adapting to Technological Advancements 105

Chapter 36: Anticipating and Managing Change 108

Chapter 37: Recap of Key Points 111

Chapter 38: Final Thoughts on the Importance of Business Culture 113

Conclusion: Call to Action: Building a Culture of Success 116

Appendix: Resources for Further Learning 119

Tools and Assessments for Analyzing Organizational Culture 121

Books: 124

Preface:

Welcome to "Importance of Business Culture," a book that explores the vital role of culture in shaping the success and sustainability of organizations in today's dynamic business world.

In the ever-evolving landscape of commerce, it has become increasingly evident that a company's culture is not just a byproduct of its operations but a driving force behind its achievements. Having spent years immersed in various organizational cultures and witnessing firsthand the transformative power of a positive culture, I embarked on a journey to delve deeper into this fascinating phenomenon.

This book is the culmination of extensive research, personal experiences, and conversations with leaders and professionals from diverse industries. It is intended to serve as a guide for individuals and organizations seeking to understand, cultivate, and leverage the power of culture to achieve their goals.

Throughout these pages, you will discover insights into the fundamental elements of business culture, the impact it has on organizational success, and strategies for nurturing a culture that fosters innovation, collaboration, and resilience. From defining core values to navigating cultural differences, from fostering diversity and inclusion to promoting a growth mindset, each chapter is designed to equip you with practical knowledge and actionable steps to cultivate a thriving workplace environment.

As you embark on this journey with me, I encourage you to approach each page with an open mind and a willingness to challenge your assumptions. Whether you are a seasoned executive, a budding entrepreneur, or an aspiring leader, my hope is that this book will inspire you to rethink the way you approach culture within your organization and empower you to drive positive change.

Thank you for joining me on this exploration of the importance of business culture. May the insights within these pages serve as a catalyst for transformation and growth in your professional journey.

Warm regards,

Laurel D. Malvern

Introduction:

Welcome to "Importance of Business Culture." In today's fast-paced and competitive business world, the concept of culture within organizations has never been more crucial. As businesses strive for success and sustainability, understanding the profound impact of culture has become essential.

In this book, we will embark on a journey to explore the multifaceted dimensions of business culture. From its fundamental elements to its role in driving innovation and collaboration, we will uncover the secrets behind building a thriving workplace environment.

Throughout these pages, I will share insights gleaned from years of research, personal experiences, and interactions with leaders across industries. Together, we will delve into the significance of culture in shaping organizational identity, values, and behaviors.

But beyond mere exploration, this book is a call to action. It is a blueprint for leaders and professionals to assess, enhance, and leverage their organization's culture for maximum impact. Whether you are a seasoned executive or a budding entrepreneur, the lessons within these pages will equip you with the tools and strategies needed to cultivate a culture of success.

Thank you for embarking on this journey with me. Let's dive into the fascinating world of business culture and unlock the keys to organizational excellence.

Warm regards,
Laurel D. Malvern

Chapter 1: Setting the Stage: Defining Business Culture

In the bustling world of business, amidst the flurry of strategies, innovations, and bottom lines, there exists a silent force that shapes the very essence of organizations: culture. But what exactly is business culture, and why does it hold such sway over the success or failure of companies?

At its core, business culture is the collective personality, values, beliefs, and behaviors that define an organization. It is the invisible thread that weaves together the fabric of an organization, guiding its decisions, actions, and interactions. From the way employees communicate to the rituals and traditions that permeate the workplace, culture manifests itself in myriad ways, shaping the experiences of everyone within the organization.

But business culture is more than just a buzzword or a feel-good concept. It is a powerful force that can make or break an organization. A positive culture fosters trust, engagement, and collaboration among employees, driving productivity, innovation, and ultimately, success. Conversely, a toxic culture marked by distrust, fear, or apathy can erode morale, stifle creativity, and lead to high turnover rates and poor performance.

To truly understand the importance of business culture, we must first recognize its multifaceted nature. Culture is not a static entity; it evolves over time, influenced by a myriad of factors, including leadership style, organizational structure, industry norms, and external forces such as societal trends and economic conditions. Moreover, culture is not confined to the walls of the office; it extends beyond, shaping how organizations interact with customers, partners, and society at large.

In this chapter, we will embark on a journey to unpack the concept of business culture, exploring its various dimensions and delving into the factors that shape and define it. Through illuminating examples and thought-provoking insights, we will gain a deeper appreciation for the pivotal role that culture plays in driving organizational success and sustainability.

So, join me as we venture into the fascinating world of business culture, where invisible forces shape the destiny of organizations and where understanding is the key to unlocking untapped potential and driving positive change.

Chapter 2: Why Business Culture Matters: Impact on Success and Sustainability

In the fast-paced and competitive landscape of modern business, achieving success and sustainability is the ultimate goal for organizations. But what sets successful companies apart from the rest? The answer often lies in the intangible yet powerful force of business culture.

Business culture matters, and it matters deeply. It is not merely a superficial aspect of organizational life but a fundamental driver of success and sustainability. In this chapter, we will delve into why business culture matters and explore its profound impact on organizations.

First and foremost, business culture shapes the identity and values of an organization. It defines who we are, what we stand for, and what we aspire to achieve. A strong culture provides a sense of purpose and direction, aligning employees around common goals and inspiring them to go above and beyond in pursuit of excellence.

Moreover, business culture plays a crucial role in driving employee engagement and retention. When employees feel connected to the values and mission of their organization, they are more likely to feel a sense of ownership and pride in their work. This, in turn, leads to higher levels of motivation, satisfaction, and loyalty, reducing turnover rates and fostering a stable and committed workforce.

But perhaps most importantly, business culture is a key determinant of organizational performance and adaptability. In today's rapidly changing business environment, organizations must be agile and innovative to stay ahead of the curve. A positive culture that encourages creativity, collaboration, and risk-taking can fuel innovation and drive continuous improvement, enabling organizations to thrive in the face of uncertainty and disruption.

Conversely, organizations with toxic cultures characterized by micromanagement, fear of failure, or resistance to change are often unable to adapt to evolving market conditions and are at risk of becoming obsolete.

In the pages that follow, we will explore real-world examples of organizations that have leveraged the power of culture to achieve remarkable success and sustainability. We will examine the strategies they have employed to cultivate a positive culture and the tangible benefits they have reaped as a result.

Through these insights, we will gain a deeper understanding of why business culture matters and how it can serve as a catalyst for organizational excellence and long-term viability. So, join me as we uncover the transformative power of culture and explore how it can propel organizations to new heights of success and sustainability.

Chapter 3: Understanding Business Culture

In the intricate tapestry of organizational life, culture stands as a defining thread, weaving together the beliefs, values, and behaviors that shape the identity of a company. To navigate this landscape effectively, it is essential to gain a deep understanding of business culture and its various dimensions.

Business culture is a multifaceted concept, encompassing a range of elements that collectively define the essence of an organization. At its core, culture reflects the shared beliefs and values that guide decision-making and behavior within the company. These values serve as the foundation upon which the organization's identity is built, shaping its interactions with employees, customers, and stakeholders alike.

Communication styles also play a significant role in shaping business culture. Whether it's the open-door policy of a startup or the hierarchical structure of a traditional corporation, the way information flows within an organization can have a profound impact on its culture. Effective communication fosters transparency, trust, and collaboration, while poor communication can lead to misunderstandings, conflicts, and a breakdown of trust.

Organizational structure is another key aspect of business culture. From flat hierarchies that promote autonomy and innovation to rigid bureaucracies that prioritize control and stability, the structure of an organization reflects its values and priorities. Understanding the underlying structure of an organization is crucial for deciphering its culture and navigating its complexities.

The work environment also plays a pivotal role in shaping business culture. Whether it's the sleek, modern offices of a tech startup or the traditional, buttoned-up atmosphere of a law firm, the physical space in which employees work can influence their attitudes, behaviors, and interactions. Creating a positive work environment that fosters creativity, collaboration, and well-being is essential for nurturing a thriving culture.

Rituals and traditions are the final piece of the puzzle when it comes to understanding business culture. From weekly team meetings to annual company retreats, these rituals serve as the glue that binds employees together and reinforces shared values and norms. By participating in these rituals, employees feel a sense of belonging and connection to the organization, strengthening its culture in the process.

In this chapter, we will explore each of these elements in depth, examining their role in shaping business culture and providing practical insights for understanding and navigating the complexities of organizational life. By gaining a deeper understanding of business culture, we can unlock the key to building thriving organizations that inspire, motivate, and empower employees to achieve their full potential.

Chapter 4: What is Business Culture?

Business culture refers to the collective values, beliefs, attitudes, and behaviors that characterize an organization and shape its identity. It encompasses the unwritten rules, norms, and customs that govern how people within the organization interact with one another, make decisions, and approach their work.

Business culture is often influenced by a variety of factors, including the organization's history, leadership style, industry, and external environment. It can be observed in various aspects of organizational life, such as communication styles, organizational structure, work environment, and rituals and traditions.

A positive business culture fosters trust, transparency, and collaboration among employees, leading to higher levels of engagement, satisfaction, and productivity. It promotes a sense of belonging and shared purpose, aligning employees around common goals and values.

Conversely, a toxic or dysfunctional business culture characterized by mistrust, resistance to change, or lack of accountability can hinder organizational performance and lead to low morale, high turnover rates, and decreased productivity.

Ultimately, business culture plays a crucial role in shaping the success and sustainability of organizations. By cultivating a positive culture that prioritizes values such as integrity, respect, and innovation, organizations can create an environment where employees thrive, and the business flourishes.

Chapter 5: Elements of Business Culture

In the intricate tapestry of organizational life, business culture is composed of various elements that collectively define the essence and character of a company. Understanding these elements is essential for gaining insight into the values, beliefs, and behaviors that shape the culture of an organization. In this chapter, we will explore the key elements of business culture and their significance in shaping organizational identity and success.

Values and Beliefs:
At the heart of every business culture are its core values and beliefs. These are the guiding principles that govern decision-making, behavior, and interactions within the organization. Whether it's a commitment to integrity, innovation, or customer service, values provide a moral compass and define what is considered important and worthy of pursuit within the organization.

Communication Styles:

Effective communication is essential for fostering transparency, trust, and collaboration within an organization. Communication styles can vary widely across different organizations, ranging from open and informal to formal and hierarchical. Understanding the prevailing communication style within an organization is crucial for navigating relationships, resolving conflicts, and achieving alignment.

Organizational Structure:

The organizational structure reflects how power, authority, and responsibilities are distributed within the organization. It can have a significant impact on the culture of an organization, influencing factors such as decision-making processes, autonomy, and accountability. Whether it's a flat hierarchy that promotes agility and innovation or a hierarchical structure that prioritizes control and stability, the organizational structure shapes the dynamics of the workplace and influences employee attitudes and behaviors.

Work Environment:

The physical space in which employees work plays a crucial role in shaping the culture of an organization. Whether it's a traditional office setting, a collaborative coworking space, or a virtual work environment, the work environment influences employee attitudes, behaviors, and interactions. Creating a positive work environment that promotes creativity, collaboration, and well-being is essential for nurturing a thriving culture.

Rituals and Traditions:

Rituals and traditions are the rituals and routines that define the daily life of an organization. From weekly team meetings to annual company retreats, these rituals serve as the glue that binds employees together and reinforces shared values and norms. By participating in these rituals, employees feel a sense of belonging and connection to the organization, strengthening its culture in the process.

By understanding and appreciating these elements of business culture, organizations can gain insights into their unique identity and values. They can then leverage these insights to cultivate a positive culture that fosters engagement, collaboration, and innovation, ultimately driving success and sustainability.

Chapter 6: Values and Beliefs

At the core of every organization's culture lie its values and beliefs. These fundamental principles serve as the moral compass that guides decision-making, shapes behavior, and defines the identity of the organization. In this chapter, we will delve into the significance of values and beliefs in shaping business culture and explore strategies for cultivating a values-driven organization.

Defining Core Values:
Core values represent the deeply held beliefs and principles that are central to the identity of an organization. They articulate what the organization stands for and serve as a guiding framework for decision-making and behavior. Whether it's integrity, innovation, or customer focus, core values provide a foundation for creating a cohesive and purpose-driven culture.
Aligning Values with Actions:

It's not enough for organizations to simply espouse a set of values; they must also align their actions with those values. This requires leaders to lead by example and ensure that organizational policies, practices, and behaviors are consistent with the stated values. When values are aligned with actions, it fosters trust, credibility, and authenticity within the organization.

Communicating Values Effectively:

Effective communication is essential for ensuring that values are understood, embraced, and lived by all members of the organization. This includes not only articulating the values through formal channels such as mission statements and employee handbooks but also embedding them into everyday conversations, decisions, and interactions. By consistently communicating the importance of values, organizations can reinforce their significance and create a shared sense of purpose and identity.

Embedding Values in Organizational Culture:

Values are not just words on a page; they are lived experiences that shape the culture of an organization. To embed values into the fabric of the culture, organizations must integrate them into every aspect of the employee experience, from recruitment and onboarding to performance management and recognition. By incorporating values into organizational rituals, traditions, and norms, organizations can reinforce their importance and create a culture that reflects and embodies those values.

Nurturing a Values-Driven Culture:

Cultivating a values-driven culture requires ongoing effort and commitment from leaders at all levels of the organization. This includes fostering open dialogue, soliciting feedback, and modeling behaviors that align with the organization's values. By creating a supportive and inclusive environment where employees feel empowered to live out the organization's values, organizations can foster a culture of trust, collaboration, and accountability.

In this chapter, we will explore these key principles and provide practical insights and strategies for cultivating a values-driven organization. By embracing and embodying their core values, organizations can create a culture that inspires and empowers employees to achieve their full potential and drive success.

Chapter 7: Communication Styles

Effective communication is the lifeblood of any organization, serving as the foundation for collaboration, coordination, and alignment. In this chapter, we will explore the various communication styles that shape business culture and examine their impact on organizational dynamics and performance.

Open and Transparent Communication:
Open communication fosters transparency, trust, and collaboration within an organization. In cultures where communication flows freely, employees feel empowered to share ideas, express concerns, and provide feedback without fear of reprisal. Leaders play a crucial role in creating an environment where open communication is valued and encouraged, setting the tone for constructive dialogue and information sharing.
Hierarchical Communication:

In organizations with hierarchical communication styles, information tends to flow vertically, following the chain of command from top to bottom. While this structure can provide clarity and direction, it may also inhibit creativity, innovation, and collaboration. Leaders must be mindful of the potential drawbacks of hierarchical communication and seek to create channels for cross-functional communication and collaboration.

Formal vs. Informal Communication:

Formal communication refers to official channels such as memos, reports, and meetings, whereas informal communication encompasses casual interactions and exchanges that occur organically within the organization. Both forms of communication have their place in business culture, but striking the right balance is key. Informal communication can foster camaraderie, build relationships, and facilitate knowledge sharing, while formal communication ensures clarity, consistency, and accountability.

Direct vs. Indirect Communication:

Direct communication is characterized by clarity, assertiveness, and straightforwardness, whereas indirect communication involves subtlety, diplomacy, and reading between the lines. Cultural differences and individual preferences may influence communication styles, making it important for employees to develop cultural competence and adapt their communication approach accordingly. Leaders can facilitate effective communication by promoting active listening, empathy, and clarity in their interactions.

Digital Communication:

With the advent of technology, digital communication has become increasingly prevalent in today's workplace. Email, instant messaging, video conferencing, and collaboration platforms offer new opportunities for communication and collaboration, but they also present challenges such as information overload, misinterpretation, and distraction. Organizations must establish clear guidelines and best practices for digital communication to ensure effectiveness, efficiency, and etiquette.

By understanding the various communication styles and their implications, organizations can foster a culture of communication that promotes transparency, collaboration, and engagement. Leaders who prioritize effective communication create an environment where employees feel valued, heard, and empowered to contribute their best ideas and efforts toward organizational success.

Chapter 8: Organizational Structure

The organizational structure serves as the backbone of any company, providing a framework for how tasks are divided, authority is distributed, and relationships are established. In this chapter, we will explore the significance of organizational structure in shaping business culture and its impact on organizational effectiveness and adaptability.

Hierarchical Structures:

Hierarchical structures are characterized by clear lines of authority and decision-making, with power concentrated at the top of the organizational hierarchy. While hierarchical structures can provide stability, clarity, and accountability, they may also hinder agility, innovation, and employee empowerment. Leaders in hierarchical organizations must balance the need for control with the imperative to foster creativity, autonomy, and collaboration.

Flat Structures:

Flat structures, on the other hand, are characterized by fewer layers of management and a greater emphasis on collaboration, flexibility, and autonomy. In flat organizations, decision-making authority is decentralized, allowing employees to take ownership of their work and contribute to organizational goals. While flat structures can foster innovation and agility, they may also present challenges in terms of coordination, communication, and accountability.

Matrix Structures:

Matrix structures combine elements of both hierarchical and flat structures, enabling organizations to balance functional expertise with cross-functional collaboration. In matrix organizations, employees report to both functional managers and project managers, allowing for greater flexibility and specialization. However, matrix structures can also lead to complexity, ambiguity, and conflicts of interest, requiring strong leadership and communication skills to navigate effectively.

Networked Structures:

Networked structures are characterized by decentralized decision-making and fluid, dynamic relationships among individuals and teams. In networked organizations, employees are empowered to collaborate across traditional boundaries and pursue opportunities for innovation and growth. While networked structures offer flexibility and adaptability, they may also lack clear direction and accountability, requiring leaders to provide guidance and support.

Organizational Culture and Structure:

The relationship between organizational culture and structure is symbiotic, with each influencing and shaping the other. A hierarchical structure may reinforce a command-and-control culture, while a flat structure may promote a culture of autonomy and empowerment. Leaders must be intentional about aligning organizational structure with culture to create a cohesive and harmonious environment that supports organizational goals and values.

By understanding the various organizational structures and their implications, leaders can design and adapt structures that promote alignment, collaboration, and agility. By fostering a culture of flexibility, innovation, and continuous improvement, organizations can thrive in today's rapidly changing business landscape.

Chapter 9: Work Environment

The work environment is more than just the physical space where employees perform their tasks; it encompasses the atmosphere, culture, and experiences that shape the daily lives of individuals within an organization. In this chapter, we will explore the significance of the work environment in shaping business culture and its impact on employee engagement, satisfaction, and performance.

Physical Workspace:
The physical workspace plays a crucial role in shaping the employee experience and influencing attitudes, behaviors, and interactions. Whether it's an open-plan office, a remote work setup, or a flexible coworking space, the design and layout of the workspace can impact productivity, collaboration, and well-being. Creating a comfortable, ergonomic, and inspiring environment fosters creativity, innovation, and engagement among employees.

Organizational Climate:
Organizational climate refers to the prevailing mood, atmosphere, and culture within an organization. It encompasses factors such as leadership style, communication patterns, and norms of behavior. A positive organizational climate is characterized by trust, respect, and psychological safety, where employees feel valued, supported, and empowered to contribute their best efforts. Leaders play a crucial role in shaping the organizational climate through their actions, behaviors, and decisions.

Work-Life Balance:
Achieving a healthy work-life balance is essential for employee well-being, satisfaction, and performance. Organizations that prioritize work-life balance offer flexible schedules, remote work options, and supportive policies and programs that enable employees to manage their personal and professional responsibilities effectively. By promoting work-life balance, organizations can reduce stress, prevent burnout, and enhance employee morale and retention.

Diversity and Inclusion:
A diverse and inclusive work environment is one where employees from diverse backgrounds, perspectives, and experiences feel valued, respected, and included. Organizations that embrace diversity and inclusion foster creativity, innovation, and collaboration, as employees bring unique insights and ideas to the table. Leaders must be intentional about creating a culture of belonging and equity, where all employees have equal opportunities to succeed and thrive.

Employee Well-being:
Employee well-being encompasses physical, mental, and emotional health and is essential for overall job satisfaction and performance. Organizations that prioritize employee well-being offer wellness programs, mental health resources, and supportive initiatives that promote resilience, self-care, and work-life balance. By investing in employee well-being, organizations can improve morale, productivity, and retention, ultimately driving organizational success.

By creating a positive work environment that promotes collaboration, well-being, and inclusion, organizations can foster a culture of engagement, innovation, and excellence. Leaders who prioritize the work environment as a strategic asset cultivate a culture where employees feel valued, motivated, and empowered to contribute their best efforts toward achieving organizational goals.

Chapter 10: Rituals and Traditions

Rituals and traditions are the ceremonial acts and routines that define the culture and identity of an organization. They serve as powerful symbols of shared values, beliefs, and norms, shaping the experiences and interactions of employees within the organization. In this chapter, we will explore the significance of rituals and traditions in business culture and their role in fostering connection, cohesion, and camaraderie.

Establishing Rituals:
Rituals are the recurring activities, ceremonies, and routines that mark significant events or milestones within an organization. Whether it's the weekly team meeting, the annual company retreat, or the monthly birthday celebrations, rituals provide a sense of continuity, belonging, and purpose. By establishing rituals, organizations create opportunities for employees to come together, connect, and bond over shared experiences.

Reinforcing Values:
Rituals and traditions serve as powerful vehicles for reinforcing the core values and beliefs of an organization. Whether it's the recognition of outstanding performance, the celebration of cultural diversity, or the commemoration of historical achievements, rituals communicate what is important and worthy of recognition within the organization. By aligning rituals with values, organizations reinforce their significance and create a culture that reflects and embodies those values.

Building Community:
Rituals and traditions play a crucial role in building a sense of community and belonging within an organization. They provide opportunities for employees to connect with one another, build relationships, and strengthen bonds of camaraderie. Whether it's the company picnic, the volunteer day, or the holiday party, rituals create spaces where employees can socialize, collaborate, and support one another, fostering a sense of unity and solidarity.

Promoting Engagement:
Rituals and traditions can also promote engagement and morale among employees by providing opportunities for recognition, celebration, and fun. Whether it's the employee of the month award, the milestone anniversary celebration, or the team-building retreat, rituals recognize and appreciate the contributions of employees, boosting morale and motivation. By fostering a culture of appreciation and celebration, organizations can inspire loyalty, commitment, and dedication among employees.

Navigating Change:
In times of change and uncertainty, rituals and traditions can serve as anchors that provide stability, continuity, and reassurance. Whether it's the farewell party for a departing colleague, the welcome lunch for a new hire, or the annual strategic planning session, rituals create rituals create spaces where employees can come together to process emotions, share experiences, and support one another through transitions. By providing a sense of continuity and connection, rituals help employees navigate change with resilience and optimism.

By embracing and celebrating rituals and traditions, organizations can foster a culture of connection, cohesion, and camaraderie. Leaders who prioritize rituals as a strategic tool cultivate a culture where employees feel valued, engaged, and empowered to contribute their best efforts toward achieving organizational goals.

Chapter 11: The Role of Business Culture in Success

In the ever-changing landscape of business, success is not solely determined by financial performance or market share. Rather, it is increasingly influenced by the intangible yet powerful force of business culture. In this chapter, we will explore the pivotal role that business culture plays in driving organizational success and sustainability.

Building Trust and Engagement:
A positive business culture fosters trust, transparency, and engagement among employees. When employees feel valued, respected, and heard, they are more likely to invest their time, energy, and creativity into their work. Trusting relationships form the foundation of effective teamwork, collaboration, and innovation, enabling organizations to achieve their goals and adapt to changing market conditions with agility and resilience.

Fostering Innovation and Creativity:
Innovation is the lifeblood of successful organizations, driving growth, differentiation, and competitive advantage. A culture that encourages experimentation, risk-taking, and learning fosters creativity and innovation among employees. By providing a supportive environment where ideas are welcomed, celebrated, and rewarded, organizations can unlock the potential of their workforce and unleash a steady stream of innovative solutions to complex challenges.

Enhancing Employee Satisfaction and Retention:
Employee satisfaction and retention are critical indicators of organizational health and performance. A positive business culture that prioritizes employee well-being, growth, and development fosters loyalty, commitment, and retention among employees. By investing in initiatives such as professional development, mentorship, and work-life balance, organizations can create an environment where employees feel valued, fulfilled, and motivated to stay and grow with the company.

Improving Collaboration and Teamwork:

Collaboration and teamwork are essential for achieving common goals and driving organizational success. A culture that values collaboration, communication, and collective problem-solving fosters strong teams and cross-functional collaboration. By breaking down silos, promoting open dialogue, and fostering a sense of belonging and ownership, organizations can harness the collective intelligence and creativity of their teams to achieve greater results together.

Driving Performance and Results:

Ultimately, business culture shapes the attitudes, behaviors, and performance of employees, influencing the overall success and sustainability of the organization. A positive culture that aligns with the organization's values, vision, and goals creates a sense of purpose, direction, and momentum that drives performance and results. By nurturing a culture of excellence, accountability, and continuous improvement, organizations can achieve their strategic objectives and thrive in today's competitive marketplace.

In conclusion, business culture is not just a nice-to-have; it is a strategic imperative for organizations seeking to achieve long-term success and sustainability. By cultivating a positive culture that values trust, innovation, collaboration, and performance, organizations can create a workplace where employees thrive, customers are delighted, and stakeholders are rewarded. Leaders who prioritize culture as a driver of success cultivate organizations that are resilient, adaptive, and poised for growth in an ever-changing world.

Chapter 12: Building Trust and Engagement

Trust and engagement are the cornerstones of a successful and thriving organization. In this chapter, we will explore the importance of building trust and fostering engagement within the workplace, and provide practical strategies for creating a culture where employees feel valued, respected, and motivated to contribute their best efforts.

Creating a Foundation of Trust:

Trust is the bedrock of any successful relationship, including those within the workplace. Leaders must demonstrate integrity, honesty, and transparency in their actions and decisions to build trust among employees. By consistently delivering on promises, being open and honest in communication, and acting with integrity, leaders can establish a culture of trust that forms the foundation for collaboration, innovation, and high performance.

Empowering Employees:

Empowering employees involves giving them the autonomy, authority, and resources they need to take ownership of their work and make meaningful contributions to the organization. Leaders must delegate responsibility, provide opportunities for growth and development, and support employees in taking calculated risks and exploring new ideas. By empowering employees to make decisions and take initiative, leaders foster a sense of ownership, accountability, and pride in their work.

Cultivating Open Communication:

Open communication is essential for building trust and fostering engagement within the workplace. Leaders must create an environment where employees feel comfortable expressing their thoughts, opinions, and concerns without fear of retribution. This involves actively listening to employees, soliciting feedback, and being responsive to their needs and concerns. By fostering open communication, leaders demonstrate respect for employees' perspectives and build trust through transparency and authenticity.

Recognizing and Appreciating Contributions:

Recognizing and appreciating employees' contributions is essential for fostering engagement and motivation within the workplace. Leaders must acknowledge and celebrate employees' achievements, both big and small, and provide meaningful recognition and rewards for their efforts. This can take the form of verbal praise, public recognition, or tangible rewards such as bonuses or promotions. By showing appreciation for employees' contributions, leaders reinforce positive behaviors and foster a culture of recognition and appreciation.

Building a Culture of Inclusivity:

Inclusive workplaces are ones where employees from diverse backgrounds, perspectives, and experiences feel valued, respected, and included. Leaders must create a culture where all employees feel welcome, heard, and empowered to bring their authentic selves to work. This involves fostering diversity and inclusion through policies, practices, and behaviors that promote equity, fairness, and belonging. By embracing diversity and fostering inclusivity, leaders create a culture where trust flourishes, engagement thrives, and innovation flourishes.

In conclusion, building trust and fostering engagement are essential for creating a workplace where employees feel valued, motivated, and empowered to contribute their best efforts. By prioritizing trust, empowerment, open communication, recognition, and inclusivity, leaders can cultivate a culture that inspires loyalty, commitment, and high performance among employees, driving organizational success and sustainability.

Chapter 13: Fostering Innovation and Creativity

Innovation and creativity are essential ingredients for organizational success in today's dynamic and competitive business environment. In this chapter, we will explore the importance of fostering innovation and creativity within the workplace and provide practical strategies for creating a culture where employees feel empowered to think creatively, experiment, and pursue new ideas.

Encouraging Risk-Taking and Experimentation:
Innovation thrives in environments where employees feel empowered to take risks, experiment, and explore new ideas. Leaders must create a culture where failure is seen as an opportunity for learning and growth rather than a mark of incompetence or inadequacy. By encouraging risk-taking and experimentation, leaders foster a culture of innovation where employees feel empowered to push boundaries, challenge the status quo, and pursue bold ideas.

Providing Resources and Support:
Innovation requires more than just creativity; it also requires resources, support, and infrastructure to bring ideas to fruition. Leaders must provide employees with access to the tools, technology, and resources they need to innovate effectively. This may involve investing in research and development, providing training and development opportunities, and fostering partnerships and collaborations with external stakeholders. By providing resources and support, leaders enable employees to turn their creative ideas into tangible solutions that drive business growth and success.

Embracing Diversity of Thought:
Diversity of thought is a powerful driver of innovation, as it brings together different perspectives, experiences, and ideas to solve complex problems and drive new opportunities. Leaders must create a culture where diversity of thought is celebrated and valued, and where employees feel encouraged to share their unique perspectives and insights. This may involve fostering diversity and inclusion through recruitment, hiring, and promotion practices, as well as creating opportunities for cross-functional collaboration and knowledge sharing. By embracing diversity of thought, leaders unlock the full potential of their workforce and drive innovation and creativity throughout the organization.

Encouraging Collaboration and Cross-Pollination:

Collaboration is essential for driving innovation, as it brings together diverse skills, expertise, and perspectives to tackle complex challenges and generate new ideas. Leaders must create opportunities for collaboration and cross-pollination across teams, departments, and disciplines. This may involve organizing brainstorming sessions, hackathons, or innovation challenges, as well as providing platforms and tools for virtual collaboration and knowledge sharing. By encouraging collaboration and cross-pollination, leaders foster a culture of innovation where ideas can flourish and grow through collective effort and collaboration.

Celebrating and Rewarding Innovation:

Finally, leaders must recognize and celebrate innovation and creativity within the organization. This may involve acknowledging and rewarding employees who contribute innovative ideas or solutions, as well as creating channels for sharing success stories and best practices. By celebrating and rewarding innovation, leaders reinforce the importance of creativity and experimentation and inspire others to pursue bold ideas and take risks.

In conclusion, fostering innovation and creativity is essential for driving organizational success and competitive advantage in today's fast-paced and ever-changing business environment. By encouraging risk-taking and experimentation, providing resources and support, embracing diversity of thought, encouraging collaboration and cross-pollination, and celebrating and rewarding innovation, leaders can create a culture where employees feel empowered to innovate, experiment, and pursue new ideas, driving continuous improvement and growth throughout the organization.

Chapter 14: Enhancing Employee Satisfaction and Retention

Employee satisfaction and retention are critical factors for organizational success, as they directly impact productivity, morale, and the bottom line. In this chapter, we will explore the importance of enhancing employee satisfaction and retention and provide practical strategies for creating a workplace where employees feel valued, engaged, and motivated to stay and grow with the organization.

Prioritizing Employee Well-being:

Employee well-being encompasses physical, mental, and emotional health and is essential for overall job satisfaction and performance. Leaders must prioritize employee well-being by offering wellness programs, mental health resources, and initiatives that promote work-life balance and stress management. By investing in employee well-being, organizations can reduce absenteeism, improve morale, and enhance employee satisfaction and retention.

Providing Opportunities for Growth and Development:
Employees are more likely to stay with an organization that offers opportunities for growth, advancement, and development. Leaders must provide employees with opportunities to learn new skills, acquire knowledge, and advance their careers through training, mentorship, and coaching programs. By investing in employee development, organizations can foster a culture of continuous learning and improvement and demonstrate their commitment to supporting employees' long-term career goals.

Creating a Positive Work Environment:
The work environment plays a crucial role in shaping employee satisfaction and retention. Leaders must create a positive work environment that fosters collaboration, creativity, and well-being. This may involve creating comfortable, ergonomic workspaces, promoting work-life balance, and fostering a culture of respect, appreciation, and inclusion. By creating a positive work environment, leaders can enhance morale, motivation, and job satisfaction among employees, leading to higher levels of retention and loyalty.

Building Strong Relationships and Trust:

Strong relationships and trust are essential for fostering employee satisfaction and retention. Leaders must build trust through open communication, transparency, and authenticity, and by demonstrating empathy, respect, and integrity in their interactions with employees. By fostering strong relationships and trust, leaders create a supportive and inclusive workplace where employees feel valued, respected, and motivated to stay and contribute their best efforts.

Recognizing and Rewarding Contributions:

Recognizing and rewarding employees' contributions is essential for fostering satisfaction and retention. Leaders must acknowledge and celebrate employees' achievements, both big and small, and provide meaningful recognition and rewards for their efforts. This may involve verbal praise, public recognition, or tangible rewards such as bonuses, promotions, or additional benefits. By showing appreciation for employees' contributions, leaders reinforce positive behaviors and create a culture of recognition and appreciation that enhances employee satisfaction and retention.

In conclusion, enhancing employee satisfaction and retention is essential for creating a workplace where employees feel valued, engaged, and motivated to stay and grow with the organization. By prioritizing employee well-being, providing opportunities for growth and development, creating a positive work environment, building strong relationships and trust, and recognizing and rewarding contributions, leaders can foster a culture of engagement, loyalty, and retention that drives organizational success and sustainability.

Chapter 15: Improving Collaboration and Teamwork

Collaboration and teamwork are essential for achieving organizational goals and driving innovation and performance. In this chapter, we will explore the importance of improving collaboration and teamwork within the workplace and provide practical strategies for creating a culture where employees work together effectively to achieve common objectives.

Fostering a Culture of Collaboration:

Collaboration flourishes in environments where employees feel empowered to share ideas, collaborate across teams, and work together toward common goals. Leaders must foster a culture of collaboration by breaking down silos, promoting open communication, and creating opportunities for cross-functional collaboration. By fostering a culture of collaboration, leaders create an environment where employees feel valued, respected, and motivated to work together to achieve shared objectives.

Providing Clear Goals and Expectations:

Clear goals and expectations are essential for guiding collaboration and ensuring alignment among team members. Leaders must communicate clear objectives, priorities, and expectations to employees, and provide regular feedback and support to help them achieve their goals. By providing clear goals and expectations, leaders create a shared understanding of what success looks like and provide a roadmap for collaboration and teamwork.

Promoting Trust and Psychological Safety:

Trust and psychological safety are foundational elements of effective collaboration and teamwork. Leaders must create an environment where employees feel comfortable taking risks, sharing ideas, and expressing dissenting opinions without fear of judgment or reprisal. This involves building trust through open communication, transparency, and authenticity, and fostering a culture of respect, empathy, and inclusion. By promoting trust and psychological safety, leaders create a supportive and empowering environment where employees can collaborate and innovate with confidence.

Encouraging Diversity of Perspectives:

Diversity of perspectives is a powerful driver of collaboration and innovation, as it brings together different ideas, experiences, and insights to solve complex problems and generate new opportunities. Leaders must encourage diversity of perspectives by fostering inclusivity, valuing diverse backgrounds and experiences, and creating opportunities for all voices to be heard. By embracing diversity of perspectives, leaders unlock the full potential of their teams and drive collaboration and innovation throughout the organization.

Providing Tools and Resources for Collaboration: Effective collaboration requires the right tools, technology, and resources to facilitate communication, coordination, and knowledge sharing among team members. Leaders must provide employees with access to collaboration tools, such as project management software, video conferencing platforms, and document sharing tools, and ensure they have the training and support they need to use them effectively. By providing tools and resources for collaboration, leaders enable teams to work together seamlessly and achieve their goals more efficiently.

In conclusion, improving collaboration and teamwork is essential for achieving organizational success and driving innovation and performance. By fostering a culture of collaboration, providing clear goals and expectations, promoting trust and psychological safety, encouraging diversity of perspectives, and providing tools and resources for collaboration, leaders can create an environment where employees work together effectively to achieve common objectives and drive organizational success.

Chapter 16: Navigating Cultural Differences

In today's globalized world, organizations often comprise diverse teams with members from different cultural backgrounds. Navigating cultural differences effectively is essential for fostering collaboration, communication, and mutual understanding within the workplace. In this chapter, we will explore the importance of navigating cultural differences and provide practical strategies for creating a culture of inclusivity and respect.

Understanding Cultural Diversity:

Cultural diversity encompasses differences in beliefs, values, customs, and behaviors among individuals from different cultural backgrounds. Leaders must recognize and appreciate the richness of cultural diversity within the workplace and understand how cultural differences can influence communication, decision-making, and collaboration. By fostering awareness and understanding of cultural diversity, leaders can create an environment where all employees feel valued, respected, and included.

Promoting Inclusivity and Respect:

Inclusivity and respect are essential for fostering a culture where employees from diverse backgrounds feel welcome, heard, and empowered to contribute their unique perspectives and insights. Leaders must promote inclusivity and respect by fostering open dialogue, valuing diverse perspectives, and creating opportunities for all voices to be heard. By creating a culture of inclusivity and respect, leaders build trust, foster collaboration, and drive innovation within the organization.

Building Cultural Competence:

Cultural competence involves developing the knowledge, skills, and awareness needed to effectively navigate cultural differences and work effectively with individuals from diverse backgrounds. Leaders must invest in building cultural competence among employees through training, education, and development programs. By equipping employees with the tools and resources they need to navigate cultural differences, leaders empower them to communicate, collaborate, and build relationships across cultures effectively.

Communicating Effectively Across Cultures:

Effective communication is essential for bridging cultural differences and fostering understanding and collaboration within diverse teams. Leaders must be mindful of cultural differences in communication styles, norms, and preferences, and adapt their communication approach accordingly. This may involve using clear and simple language, avoiding jargon or slang, and being sensitive to nonverbal cues and gestures. By communicating effectively across cultures, leaders build trust, minimize misunderstandings, and foster positive relationships within the workplace.

Embracing Cultural Diversity as a Strength:

Cultural diversity is not just a challenge to be managed; it is also a source of strength and innovation within the organization. Leaders must embrace cultural diversity as a strategic asset and leverage the unique perspectives and insights of employees from diverse backgrounds to drive creativity, innovation, and competitive advantage. By fostering a culture where diversity is celebrated and valued, leaders create an environment where employees feel empowered to bring their whole selves to work and contribute their best ideas and efforts toward organizational success.

In conclusion, navigating cultural differences effectively is essential for fostering collaboration, communication, and mutual understanding within diverse teams. By promoting inclusivity and respect, building cultural competence, communicating effectively across cultures, and embracing cultural diversity as a strength, leaders can create a culture where all employees feel valued, respected, and empowered to contribute their unique perspectives and insights toward achieving common goals and driving organizational success.

Chapter 17: Globalization and Cultural Diversity in Business

Globalization has transformed the business landscape, bringing together individuals and organizations from diverse cultural backgrounds and geographical locations. In this chapter, we will explore the impact of globalization on cultural diversity in business and provide insights into how organizations can leverage cultural diversity as a strategic advantage in today's interconnected world.

The Impact of Globalization:
Globalization has led to increased interconnectedness and interdependence among economies, societies, and cultures worldwide. Organizations operate in a global marketplace characterized by diverse customer preferences, regulatory environments, and business practices. As a result, cultural diversity has become a defining feature of the modern business landscape, presenting both challenges and opportunities for organizations seeking to navigate global markets.

Embracing Cultural Diversity:
Embracing cultural diversity is essential for organizations seeking to thrive in today's globalized world. Leaders must recognize and appreciate the value of cultural diversity in driving innovation, creativity, and competitive advantage within the organization. By embracing cultural diversity, organizations can tap into the unique perspectives, insights, and talents of employees from diverse backgrounds to develop innovative solutions, enter new markets, and better serve diverse customer segments.

Leveraging Cultural Intelligence:
Cultural intelligence (CQ) refers to the ability to adapt and interact effectively across different cultural contexts. Leaders must develop cultural intelligence among employees by fostering awareness, understanding, and empathy for cultural differences. This involves providing cultural competency training, promoting cross-cultural collaboration, and creating opportunities for employees to gain exposure to diverse cultural perspectives and experiences. By leveraging cultural intelligence, organizations can build strong relationships, navigate cultural differences, and drive collaboration and innovation across global teams.

Developing Inclusive Global Leadership:

Inclusive global leadership is essential for fostering a culture of inclusivity, respect, and belonging within diverse global teams. Leaders must demonstrate inclusive leadership behaviors such as empathy, openness, and cultural sensitivity, and create a culture where all employees feel valued, respected, and empowered to contribute their unique perspectives and talents. This involves promoting diversity in leadership roles, providing opportunities for global mobility and career development, and fostering a culture of collaboration and teamwork across geographical boundaries.

Navigating Cross-Cultural Challenges:

Despite the benefits of cultural diversity, organizations may encounter challenges when operating in global markets, including language barriers, communication misunderstandings, and cultural differences in business practices and norms. Leaders must be proactive in addressing cross-cultural challenges by fostering open dialogue, promoting cultural awareness and sensitivity, and providing support and resources to help employees navigate cultural differences effectively. By addressing cross-cultural challenges, organizations can build trust, minimize misunderstandings, and foster positive relationships with stakeholders in global markets.

In conclusion, globalization has made cultural diversity a fundamental aspect of business in the 21st century. By embracing cultural diversity, leveraging cultural intelligence, developing inclusive global leadership, and navigating cross-cultural challenges effectively, organizations can harness the power of cultural diversity to drive innovation, collaboration, and success in today's interconnected and diverse global marketplace.

Chapter 18: Challenges and Opportunities of Cross-Cultural Communication

Cross-cultural communication is both a challenge and an opportunity for organizations operating in today's globalized world. In this chapter, we will explore the complexities of cross-cultural communication, highlight common challenges, and provide strategies for leveraging cultural differences to enhance communication and collaboration within diverse teams.

Understanding Cultural Differences:
Cultural differences encompass a wide range of factors including language, communication styles, values, customs, and social norms. Misunderstandings can arise when individuals from different cultural backgrounds interpret communication cues differently. Leaders must foster awareness and understanding of cultural differences among team members to mitigate potential challenges and promote effective cross-cultural communication.

Language Barriers:
Language barriers pose a significant challenge to effective cross-cultural communication, particularly in multicultural teams where members may have varying levels of proficiency in a common language. Leaders must be proactive in addressing language barriers by providing language training, translation services, and opportunities for language exchange and practice. By promoting language proficiency among team members, organizations can enhance communication and collaboration across cultural boundaries.

Nonverbal Communication:
Nonverbal communication, including body language, facial expressions, and gestures, varies across cultures and can convey different meanings and interpretations. Leaders must be mindful of nonverbal cues and adapt their communication style to accommodate cultural differences. This may involve seeking clarification, practicing active listening, and demonstrating empathy and cultural sensitivity in interactions with team members from diverse cultural backgrounds.

High-Context vs. Low-Context Cultures:
Cultural differences in communication styles can be categorized as high-context or low-context cultures. High-context cultures rely on implicit communication cues and context to convey meaning, whereas low-context cultures emphasize explicit communication and rely on verbal expression. Leaders must be aware of cultural differences in communication styles and adapt their approach accordingly to ensure messages are effectively conveyed and understood across cultural boundaries.

Cultivating Cultural Intelligence:
Cultural intelligence (CQ) refers to the ability to adapt and interact effectively across different cultural contexts. Leaders must cultivate cultural intelligence among team members by providing cultural competency training, promoting cross-cultural awareness, and creating opportunities for exposure to diverse cultural perspectives and experiences. By fostering cultural intelligence, organizations can enhance communication and collaboration within diverse teams and leverage cultural differences as a source of strength and innovation.

Leveraging Diversity as a Strength:
Despite the challenges of cross-cultural communication, organizations can leverage cultural diversity as a strategic advantage by promoting inclusivity, respect, and understanding within the workplace. Leaders must create a culture where all employees feel valued, respected, and empowered to contribute their unique perspectives and talents. By embracing cultural diversity and fostering a culture of inclusivity, organizations can enhance communication and collaboration, drive innovation, and achieve sustainable success in today's globalized world.

In conclusion, cross-cultural communication presents both challenges and opportunities for organizations operating in diverse and multicultural environments. By understanding cultural differences, addressing language barriers, adapting communication styles, cultivating cultural intelligence, and leveraging diversity as a strength, organizations can enhance communication and collaboration within diverse teams and drive success in today's interconnected and globalized business landscape.

Chapter 19: Strategies for Managing Cultural Differences

Effectively managing cultural differences is essential for fostering collaboration, communication, and success within diverse teams and organizations. In this chapter, we will explore practical strategies for navigating cultural differences and promoting inclusivity, respect, and understanding within the workplace.

Foster Cultural Awareness and Sensitivity:
Cultivating cultural awareness and sensitivity is the foundation for effectively managing cultural differences within the workplace. Leaders must provide cultural competency training and education to help employees understand and appreciate the perspectives, values, and customs of colleagues from diverse cultural backgrounds. By fostering cultural awareness and sensitivity, organizations create a culture of inclusivity and respect that promotes effective communication and collaboration.
Encourage Open Dialogue and Communication:
Open dialogue and communication are essential for addressing cultural differences and fostering understanding within diverse teams. Leaders must create a safe and supportive environment where employees feel comfortable discussing cultural differences, sharing experiences, and asking questions. By encouraging open dialogue and communication, organizations can build trust, minimize misunderstandings, and promote collaboration and teamwork across cultural boundaries.
Promote Cross-Cultural Collaboration and Teamwork:

Cross-cultural collaboration and teamwork are essential for leveraging the diverse perspectives and talents of employees from different cultural backgrounds. Leaders must create opportunities for cross-cultural collaboration by forming diverse teams, promoting intercultural exchanges, and facilitating cross-cultural training and development programs. By promoting cross-cultural collaboration and teamwork, organizations can drive innovation, creativity, and performance within diverse teams.

Adapt Communication Styles and Practices:

Cultural differences in communication styles and practices can lead to misunderstandings and miscommunication within diverse teams. Leaders must be mindful of cultural differences and adapt their communication style and practices to accommodate the preferences and norms of colleagues from different cultural backgrounds. This may involve using clear and simple language, avoiding jargon or slang, and being sensitive to nonverbal cues and gestures. By adapting communication styles and practices, leaders can enhance communication and collaboration within diverse teams.

Establish Common Goals and Values:

Establishing common goals and values helps to unite employees from diverse cultural backgrounds and create a shared sense of purpose and identity within the organization. Leaders must articulate clear goals and values that resonate with employees across cultural boundaries and foster a culture of inclusivity, respect, and collaboration. By establishing common goals and values, organizations can align the efforts of diverse teams and drive collective action toward shared objectives.

Lead by Example:

Leaders play a crucial role in setting the tone and expectations for managing cultural differences within the workplace. Leaders must lead by example by demonstrating cultural awareness, sensitivity, and inclusivity in their actions and behaviors. This involves promoting diversity in leadership roles, valuing diverse perspectives, and creating opportunities for all employees to contribute their unique talents and insights. By leading by example, leaders inspire trust, foster collaboration, and create a culture where all employees feel valued, respected, and empowered to succeed.

In conclusion, effectively managing cultural differences requires proactive efforts to foster cultural awareness, promote open dialogue and communication, encourage cross-cultural collaboration and teamwork, adapt communication styles and practices, establish common goals and values, and lead by example. By implementing these strategies, organizations can create a culture of inclusivity, respect, and understanding that fosters collaboration, innovation, and success within diverse teams and across global markets.

Chapter 20: Creating a Positive Business Culture

A positive business culture is the cornerstone of organizational success, fostering employee engagement, productivity, and well-being. In this chapter, we will explore the key components of a positive business culture and provide practical strategies for creating an environment where employees thrive and the organization flourishes.

Define Core Values and Behaviors:
Core values serve as the guiding principles that shape the culture and identity of an organization. Leaders must define clear and meaningful core values that reflect the organization's mission, vision, and aspirations. These values should be translated into actionable behaviors that guide decision-making, interactions, and behaviors at all levels of the organization. By defining core values and behaviors, leaders set the foundation for a positive business culture built on integrity, respect, and accountability.

Promote Trust and Transparency:
Trust and transparency are essential for fostering a positive business culture where employees feel valued, respected, and empowered. Leaders must communicate openly and honestly with employees, sharing information about the organization's goals, priorities, and challenges. By promoting trust and transparency, leaders build credibility, inspire confidence, and foster a culture of openness, collaboration, and accountability.

Cultivate a Growth Mindset:

A growth mindset is essential for fostering a culture of continuous learning, improvement, and innovation. Leaders must cultivate a growth mindset among employees by promoting a willingness to learn, adapt, and embrace challenges and failures as opportunities for growth and development. This involves providing opportunities for training, development, and mentorship, and celebrating learning and achievement. By cultivating a growth mindset, leaders inspire resilience, creativity, and adaptability within the organization.

Foster Collaboration and Teamwork:

Collaboration and teamwork are essential for achieving organizational goals and driving innovation and performance. Leaders must create opportunities for collaboration by promoting open communication, trust, and mutual respect among team members. This may involve organizing cross-functional teams, promoting knowledge sharing and collaboration tools, and recognizing and rewarding collaborative efforts. By fostering collaboration and teamwork, leaders create a culture where employees feel supported, empowered, and motivated to work together toward common objectives.

Prioritize Employee Well-being:

Employee well-being is fundamental to a positive business culture, as it directly impacts engagement, productivity, and retention. Leaders must prioritize employee well-being by promoting work-life balance, providing resources and support for physical and mental health, and creating a culture where employees feel valued and supported. This may involve offering wellness programs, flexible work arrangements, and opportunities for stress management and relaxation. By prioritizing employee well-being, leaders create a culture of care, compassion, and resilience within the organization.

Celebrate Success and Recognize Contributions:

Celebrating success and recognizing employees' contributions is essential for fostering a culture of appreciation and motivation within the organization. Leaders must acknowledge and celebrate achievements, milestones, and successes, both big and small. This may involve public recognition, rewards, and incentives, as well as creating opportunities for employees to share their successes and accomplishments with their colleagues. By celebrating success and recognizing contributions, leaders reinforce positive behaviors, foster a sense of pride and belonging, and inspire continued excellence within the organization.

In conclusion, creating a positive business culture requires proactive efforts to define core values and behaviors, promote trust and transparency, cultivate a growth mindset, foster collaboration and teamwork, prioritize employee well-being, and celebrate success and recognize contributions. By implementing these strategies, leaders can create an environment where employees feel valued, engaged, and empowered to contribute their best efforts toward achieving organizational goals and driving sustainable success.

Chapter 21: Leadership's Role in Shaping Culture

Leadership plays a pivotal role in shaping the culture of an organization, influencing its values, norms, and behaviors. In this chapter, we will explore the importance of leadership in shaping culture and provide insights into how leaders can foster a positive and thriving organizational culture.

Setting the Tone:
Leaders set the tone for organizational culture through their words, actions, and behaviors. They must lead by example, embodying the values and principles they wish to instill within the organization. Leaders who demonstrate integrity, authenticity, and humility inspire trust and confidence among employees, fostering a culture of openness, transparency, and accountability.
Articulating Vision and Values:
Leaders must articulate a compelling vision and set of values that inspire and guide employees in their daily work. They must communicate the organization's mission, vision, and values clearly and consistently, ensuring alignment and commitment from all stakeholders. By articulating a clear and compelling vision, leaders provide a sense of purpose and direction that guides decision-making and behaviors throughout the organization.
Fostering Trust and Empowerment:

Trust is the foundation of effective leadership and organizational culture. Leaders must foster trust by building relationships, demonstrating competence, and acting with integrity and transparency. They must empower employees by delegating authority, providing autonomy, and creating opportunities for growth and development. By fostering trust and empowerment, leaders create a culture where employees feel valued, respected, and motivated to contribute their best efforts.

Promoting Diversity and Inclusion:

Leaders must promote diversity and inclusion within the organization by creating a culture where all voices are heard, valued, and respected. They must champion diversity in leadership roles, promote inclusive hiring and promotion practices, and create opportunities for diverse perspectives to be heard and valued. By promoting diversity and inclusion, leaders foster innovation, creativity, and collaboration within the organization.

Driving Accountability and Performance:

Leaders must drive accountability and performance by setting clear expectations, providing feedback and support, and holding employees accountable for results. They must create a culture of high performance by recognizing and rewarding excellence, addressing performance issues promptly and effectively, and promoting a growth mindset that values continuous learning and improvement. By driving accountability and performance, leaders create a culture of excellence and achievement that drives organizational success.

Nurturing Continuous Learning and Adaptation:

In today's rapidly changing business environment, leaders must foster a culture of continuous learning and adaptation. They must encourage experimentation, risk-taking, and innovation, and create opportunities for employees to develop new skills and adapt to change. By nurturing continuous learning and adaptation, leaders ensure that the organization remains agile, resilient, and competitive in the face of uncertainty and disruption.

In conclusion, leadership plays a critical role in shaping the culture of an organization. By setting the tone, articulating vision and values, fostering trust and empowerment, promoting diversity and inclusion, driving accountability and performance, and nurturing continuous learning and adaptation, leaders can create a positive and thriving organizational culture that inspires excellence, innovation, and success.

Chapter 22: Establishing Core Values and Mission

Establishing core values and a clear mission statement is fundamental for shaping the culture and direction of an organization. In this chapter, we delve into the significance of defining core values and mission and provide guidance on how leaders can create a compelling framework that guides the organization's actions and decisions.

Defining Core Values:
Core values represent the fundamental beliefs and principles that guide the behavior and decision-making of individuals within an organization. Leaders must engage stakeholders to identify and define core values that reflect the organization's identity, culture, and aspirations. These values should be timeless, enduring, and actionable, serving as the foundation for the organization's culture and guiding principles.

Articulating a Clear Mission:
A mission statement articulates the purpose and raison d'être of the organization, clarifying its goals, objectives, and intended impact. Leaders must craft a concise and compelling mission statement that communicates the organization's unique value proposition and its commitment to serving stakeholders. This statement should inspire and motivate employees, aligning their efforts and actions with the organization's broader purpose and objectives.

Aligning Values with Actions:

It is not enough to define core values and articulate a mission; leaders must also ensure alignment between these values and the organization's actions and behaviors. Leaders must lead by example, embodying the values and principles they wish to instill within the organization. They must integrate core values into all aspects of the organization, from hiring and onboarding to performance management and decision-making processes.

Communicating Values and Mission:

Effective communication is essential for ensuring that core values and mission resonate with employees and stakeholders. Leaders must communicate core values and mission through various channels, including internal communications, training programs, and organizational events. By consistently reinforcing core values and mission, leaders cultivate a shared understanding and commitment among employees, driving alignment and engagement throughout the organization.

Embedding Values and Mission into Culture:

Core values and mission should not be static statements; they should evolve and adapt to reflect changes in the organization's environment and strategic priorities. Leaders must embed core values and mission into the organization's culture, ensuring that they inform decision-making, shape behaviors, and drive organizational performance. This may involve integrating values and mission into performance management systems, recognition programs, and employee development initiatives.

Evaluating and Evolving:

Finally, leaders must regularly evaluate the effectiveness of core values and mission in guiding the organization's actions and decisions. They must solicit feedback from employees and stakeholders, assess alignment with organizational goals and objectives, and identify opportunities for improvement and refinement. By continuously evaluating and evolving core values and mission, leaders ensure that they remain relevant, impactful, and reflective of the organization's identity and aspirations.

In conclusion, establishing core values and mission is essential for shaping the culture and direction of an organization. By defining core values, articulating a clear mission, aligning values with actions, communicating effectively, embedding values and mission into culture, and evaluating and evolving over time, leaders can create a compelling framework that guides the organization's actions and decisions, inspires employees, and drives organizational success.

Chapter 23: Promoting Diversity, Equity, and Inclusion

Promoting diversity, equity, and inclusion (DEI) is not only a moral imperative but also a strategic imperative for organizations seeking to foster innovation, creativity, and sustainable growth. In this chapter, we explore the importance of DEI in creating a positive and inclusive organizational culture and provide strategies for promoting diversity, equity, and inclusion within the workplace.

Understanding Diversity:
Diversity encompasses the range of human differences, including but not limited to race, ethnicity, gender, sexual orientation, age, disability, socioeconomic status, and cultural background. Leaders must recognize and appreciate the value of diversity in bringing together different perspectives, experiences, and insights to drive innovation and performance within the organization.

Embracing Inclusion:
Inclusion involves creating a culture where all individuals feel valued, respected, and empowered to contribute their unique talents and perspectives. Leaders must foster inclusion by promoting a sense of belonging, providing opportunities for diverse voices to be heard, and addressing barriers to participation and advancement. By embracing inclusion, organizations unlock the full potential of their diverse workforce and drive collaboration and innovation.

Advancing Equity:

Equity involves ensuring fair and equal access to opportunities, resources, and support for all individuals, regardless of background or identity. Leaders must advance equity by identifying and addressing systemic barriers and biases that may disproportionately impact certain groups within the organization. This may involve implementing policies and practices to promote pay equity, diverse hiring and promotion practices, and providing resources and support for underrepresented groups.

Creating a Culture of Belonging:

A culture of belonging is essential for fostering engagement, retention, and satisfaction among employees. Leaders must create an environment where all individuals feel welcomed, valued, and included, regardless of background or identity. This may involve promoting cultural awareness and sensitivity, providing training and education on unconscious bias, and fostering relationships and networks that support belonging and connection.

Empowering Employee Resource Groups:

Employee resource groups (ERGs) provide a platform for employees from underrepresented groups to connect, share experiences, and advocate for change within the organization. Leaders must empower ERGs by providing resources, support, and recognition for their efforts, and actively engaging with them to address DEI challenges and opportunities. By empowering ERGs, organizations harness the collective power of diverse voices and perspectives to drive meaningful change and progress.

Holding Leaders Accountable:

Leaders play a critical role in driving DEI efforts within the organization. They must lead by example, demonstrating a commitment to diversity, equity, and inclusion in their actions and behaviors. Leaders must hold themselves and others accountable for promoting DEI, setting clear expectations, and measuring progress toward DEI goals and objectives. By holding leaders accountable, organizations create a culture where DEI is prioritized and integrated into all aspects of the business.

In conclusion, promoting diversity, equity, and inclusion is essential for creating a positive and inclusive organizational culture that drives innovation, engagement, and performance. By embracing diversity, fostering inclusion, advancing equity, creating a culture of belonging, empowering employee resource groups, and holding leaders accountable, organizations can build a diverse and inclusive workplace where all individuals feel valued, respected, and empowered to succeed.

Chapter 24: Cultivating a Growth Mindset

A growth mindset is the belief that one's abilities and intelligence can be developed through dedication, effort, and perseverance. Cultivating a growth mindset is essential for fostering resilience, learning, and continuous improvement within the organization. In this chapter, we explore the importance of cultivating a growth mindset and provide strategies for promoting a culture of growth and development.

Understanding the Growth Mindset:
A growth mindset is characterized by a belief in the power of effort and learning to improve one's abilities and achieve success. Individuals with a growth mindset embrace challenges, persist in the face of setbacks, and see failures as opportunities for growth and learning. Leaders must foster a growth mindset within the organization by promoting a culture where mistakes are viewed as learning opportunities and effort is celebrated as the pathway to success.

Embracing Challenges:
Challenges are opportunities for growth and development. Leaders must encourage employees to embrace challenges, step outside their comfort zones, and take calculated risks in pursuit of their goals. By promoting a culture where challenges are viewed as opportunities for growth, leaders inspire resilience, creativity, and innovation within the organization.

Learning from Failure:

Failure is an inevitable part of the learning process. Leaders must create an environment where employees feel safe to take risks, experiment, and learn from failure. They must encourage employees to reflect on their experiences, identify lessons learned, and apply them to future endeavors. By promoting a culture where failure is normalized and celebrated as a stepping stone to success, leaders foster resilience and growth within the organization.

Providing Opportunities for Development:

Continuous learning and development are essential for cultivating a growth mindset within the organization. Leaders must provide employees with opportunities for training, education, and skill development to support their professional growth and advancement. This may involve offering workshops, seminars, and online courses, as well as providing mentorship and coaching programs. By investing in employee development, leaders empower employees to reach their full potential and contribute their best efforts to the organization.

Offering Constructive Feedback:

Feedback is essential for growth and improvement. Leaders must provide employees with regular, constructive feedback that helps them understand their strengths and areas for development. Feedback should be specific, actionable, and delivered in a supportive and encouraging manner. By offering constructive feedback, leaders help employees identify opportunities for growth and development and support their ongoing learning journey.

Celebrating Progress and Achievement:

Celebrating progress and achievement is essential for reinforcing a growth mindset within the organization. Leaders must recognize and celebrate employees' efforts and accomplishments, both big and small. This may involve public recognition, rewards, and incentives, as well as creating opportunities for employees to share their successes and achievements with their colleagues. By celebrating progress and achievement, leaders reinforce the importance of effort and perseverance in achieving success and inspire continued growth and development within the organization.

In conclusion, cultivating a growth mindset is essential for fostering resilience, learning, and continuous improvement within the organization. By embracing challenges, learning from failure, providing opportunities for development, offering constructive feedback, and celebrating progress and achievement, leaders can create a culture where employees feel empowered to embrace growth and reach their full potential.

Chapter 25: Encouraging Work-Life Balance

Work-life balance is essential for promoting employee well-being, productivity, and satisfaction. In this chapter, we explore the importance of encouraging work-life balance and provide strategies for creating a supportive environment where employees can thrive both professionally and personally.

Recognizing the Importance of Work-Life Balance:
Work-life balance is the equilibrium between work-related responsibilities and personal activities, such as family time, hobbies, and self-care. Leaders must recognize the importance of work-life balance in promoting employee health, happiness, and overall well-being. By prioritizing work-life balance, organizations can reduce stress, prevent burnout, and enhance employee engagement and retention.

Setting Clear Expectations:
Clear expectations are essential for promoting work-life balance within the organization. Leaders must establish clear guidelines and boundaries around work hours, availability, and expectations for responsiveness outside of regular working hours. By setting clear expectations, leaders empower employees to manage their time effectively and prioritize their personal well-being.

Encouraging Flexible Work Arrangements:

Flexible work arrangements, such as telecommuting, flexible hours, and compressed workweeks, can provide employees with greater autonomy and control over their work schedules. Leaders must encourage and support flexible work arrangements that accommodate employees' individual needs and preferences. By offering flexibility, organizations can attract and retain top talent, improve employee satisfaction, and enhance work-life balance.

Promoting Time Management and Prioritization:

Effective time management and prioritization skills are essential for maintaining work-life balance. Leaders must provide employees with training and resources to help them manage their time effectively, set realistic goals, and prioritize tasks based on importance and urgency. By promoting time management and prioritization skills, leaders empower employees to achieve work-life balance while maximizing their productivity and performance.

Creating a Culture of Wellness:

Wellness programs and initiatives can play a crucial role in promoting work-life balance and supporting employee well-being. Leaders must create a culture of wellness by offering resources and support for physical, mental, and emotional health. This may involve providing access to fitness facilities, wellness workshops, counseling services, and employee assistance programs. By prioritizing employee wellness, organizations demonstrate a commitment to supporting work-life balance and promoting a healthy and thriving workforce.

Leading by Example:

Leaders must lead by example by prioritizing their own work-life balance and demonstrating healthy work habits to their team members. Leaders should model behaviors such as taking regular breaks, setting boundaries around work hours, and prioritizing time for personal activities and self-care. By leading by example, leaders create a culture where work-life balance is valued and supported at all levels of the organization.

In conclusion, encouraging work-life balance is essential for promoting employee well-being, productivity, and satisfaction. By setting clear expectations, encouraging flexible work arrangements, promoting time management and prioritization skills, creating a culture of wellness, and leading by example, leaders can create a supportive environment where employees can thrive both personally and professionally.

Chapter 26: Case Studies: Exemplary Business Cultures

In this chapter, we will examine case studies of organizations that have established exemplary business cultures, fostering innovation, employee engagement, and sustainable growth. By analyzing these case studies, we can glean insights and best practices for creating a positive and thriving organizational culture.

Google:
Google is renowned for its distinctive organizational culture, characterized by innovation, creativity, and employee empowerment. Google fosters a culture of collaboration and experimentation, encouraging employees to pursue ambitious projects and think outside the box. Through initiatives such as "20% time," where employees are encouraged to dedicate a portion of their workweek to pursuing passion projects, Google promotes autonomy, creativity, and intrinsic motivation among its workforce. By prioritizing employee well-being through perks such as free meals, on-site wellness facilities, and flexible work arrangements, Google demonstrates a commitment to supporting work-life balance and employee satisfaction.

Zappos:

Zappos is celebrated for its unique culture, centered around delivering exceptional customer service and cultivating a fun and vibrant workplace environment. Zappos prioritizes employee happiness and engagement, recognizing that satisfied employees are more likely to deliver exceptional service to customers. Through initiatives such as the "Zappos Culture Book," where employees contribute stories and testimonials about the company's culture and values, Zappos reinforces a sense of belonging and shared purpose among its workforce. By offering perks such as unlimited vacation time and a zany office environment, Zappos creates a culture where employees feel valued, empowered, and motivated to deliver their best work.

Patagonia:

Patagonia is renowned for its commitment to environmental sustainability and social responsibility, reflected in its unique organizational culture. Patagonia fosters a culture of environmental stewardship and activism, empowering employees to take action on issues they care about. Through initiatives such as the "1% for the Planet" program, where Patagonia donates 1% of its sales to environmental causes, the company demonstrates a commitment to making a positive impact on the planet. By offering perks such as on-site childcare, flexible work schedules, and paid time off for volunteering, Patagonia prioritizes employee well-being and work-life balance, fostering a culture where employees are motivated to align their personal values with their work.

Southwest Airlines:

Southwest Airlines is renowned for its unique culture, characterized by a spirit of fun, teamwork, and customer service excellence. Southwest fosters a culture of employee engagement and empowerment, recognizing that satisfied employees are more likely to deliver exceptional service to customers. Through initiatives such as the "Southwest Family Assistance Fund," where employees can apply for financial assistance in times of need, Southwest demonstrates a commitment to supporting employee well-being and resilience. By offering perks such as profit-sharing, generous travel benefits, and a supportive work environment, Southwest creates a culture where employees feel valued, motivated, and proud to be part of the Southwest family.

In conclusion, these case studies illustrate the power of organizational culture in driving innovation, employee engagement, and sustainable growth. By prioritizing values such as autonomy, creativity, employee well-being, and social responsibility, organizations can create a positive and thriving culture that attracts top talent, fosters innovation, and delivers exceptional results.

Chapter 27: Companies That Have Successfully Nurtured a Positive Culture

In this chapter, we will explore companies that have successfully nurtured a positive culture, fostering an environment where employees feel valued, engaged, and empowered to thrive. By examining the practices and strategies of these companies, we can gain insights into what it takes to cultivate a culture of success and satisfaction.

Salesforce:
Salesforce is renowned for its commitment to creating a culture of equality, trust, and innovation. The company prioritizes diversity, equity, and inclusion (DEI) initiatives, with programs such as "Equality for All" and "Trailblazer Community" aimed at promoting diversity and empowering underrepresented groups. Salesforce fosters a culture of trust and transparency, with CEO Marc Benioff leading by example through initiatives such as the "Ohana Culture," which emphasizes family-like values and a sense of belonging among employees. By offering perks such as paid volunteer time off, generous parental leave policies, and opportunities for career development and advancement, Salesforce demonstrates a commitment to supporting employee well-being and professional growth.
Microsoft:

Microsoft is celebrated for its transformational journey under the leadership of CEO Satya Nadella, who has prioritized culture change and employee empowerment since taking the helm in 2014. Nadella has focused on fostering a growth mindset culture, encouraging employees to embrace learning, experimentation, and innovation. Microsoft promotes diversity and inclusion through initiatives such as the "Diversity and Inclusion Dashboard," which tracks progress and accountability on DEI goals. By investing in employee development and well-being through initiatives such as the "Growth Mindset Inclusion Model" and "Employee Assistance Program," Microsoft creates a culture where employees feel valued, supported, and motivated to contribute their best work.

Airbnb:

Airbnb is renowned for its unique culture, characterized by a sense of belonging, authenticity, and community. The company fosters a culture of belonging through initiatives such as the "Belonging at Airbnb" program, which promotes diversity, equity, and inclusion through employee resource groups and allyship training. Airbnb prioritizes employee well-being and work-life balance through initiatives such as the "Wellness Program" and "Flexible Time Off" policy, which empower employees to prioritize their health and personal interests. By fostering a culture of authenticity and transparency, Airbnb creates a supportive environment where employees feel empowered to bring their whole selves to work and make a positive impact on the world.

Netflix:

Netflix is renowned for its unique culture, characterized by freedom, responsibility, and a relentless focus on innovation. The company fosters a culture of freedom and responsibility through initiatives such as the "Freedom and Responsibility Culture Deck," which outlines the company's values and expectations for employees. Netflix promotes employee empowerment and autonomy through initiatives such as the "No Rules Policy," which encourages employees to take ownership of their work and make decisions based on what is best for the company. By offering perks such as unlimited vacation time, flexible work arrangements, and generous parental leave policies, Netflix demonstrates a commitment to supporting employee well-being and work-life balance.

In conclusion, these companies exemplify the power of nurturing a positive culture to drive success, satisfaction, and sustainable growth. By prioritizing values such as diversity, equity, inclusion, trust, empowerment, and well-being, these companies create environments where employees feel valued, engaged, and motivated to contribute their best work.

Chapter 28: Lessons Learned from Their Journeys

The journeys of companies that have successfully nurtured positive cultures offer valuable lessons for organizations seeking to create environments where employees thrive. In this chapter, we distill key lessons learned from their experiences, providing actionable insights for cultivating a culture of success and satisfaction.

Prioritize Diversity, Equity, and Inclusion (DEI):
Companies that prioritize diversity, equity, and inclusion (DEI) create environments where all individuals feel valued, respected, and empowered to contribute their unique perspectives and talents. Lessons learned from companies such as Salesforce and Airbnb demonstrate the importance of investing in DEI initiatives, promoting allyship, and creating a sense of belonging among employees.

Foster a Growth Mindset Culture:
Cultivating a growth mindset culture is essential for driving innovation, learning, and continuous improvement within the organization. Lessons learned from companies such as Microsoft and Netflix emphasize the importance of promoting a growth mindset, encouraging employees to embrace challenges, learn from failure, and pursue personal and professional development opportunities.

Empower Employees and Promote Autonomy:

Empowering employees and promoting autonomy fosters a sense of ownership, accountability, and motivation within the organization. Lessons learned from companies such as Netflix and Google highlight the importance of providing employees with the freedom to make decisions, take risks, and innovate without fear of failure. By trusting employees to take ownership of their work and make decisions based on what is best for the company, organizations can unlock the full potential of their workforce and drive sustainable growth.

Support Employee Well-being and Work-Life Balance:
Supporting employee well-being and promoting work-life balance is essential for fostering engagement, satisfaction, and retention within the organization. Lessons learned from companies such as Airbnb and Salesforce underscore the importance of prioritizing employee well-being, offering perks such as flexible work arrangements, paid time off, and wellness programs to support employees' physical, mental, and emotional health.

Lead by Example and Create a Culture of Trust:
Leaders play a critical role in shaping organizational culture and driving success. Lessons learned from companies such as Salesforce and Microsoft emphasize the importance of leading by example, demonstrating integrity, authenticity, and humility in their actions and behaviors. By creating a culture of trust, transparency, and accountability, leaders inspire confidence, foster collaboration, and create environments where employees feel valued, respected, and empowered to succeed.

Embrace Continuous Learning and Adaptation:

Organizations must embrace continuous learning and adaptation to remain agile, resilient, and competitive in today's rapidly changing business environment. Lessons learned from companies such as Microsoft and Airbnb highlight the importance of fostering a culture of experimentation, innovation, and adaptation. By encouraging employees to embrace change, learn from experience, and continuously improve, organizations can drive innovation, creativity, and sustainable growth.

In conclusion, the journeys of companies that have successfully nurtured positive cultures offer valuable lessons for organizations seeking to create environments where employees thrive. By prioritizing diversity, equity, and inclusion, fostering a growth mindset culture, empowering employees, supporting well-being and work-life balance, leading by example, and embracing continuous learning and adaptation, organizations can cultivate cultures of success, satisfaction, and sustainable growth.

Chapter 29: Assessing and Improving Your Business Culture

Assessing and improving your business culture is essential for fostering a positive and thriving workplace environment. In this chapter, we will explore strategies for evaluating your organization's culture, identifying areas for improvement, and implementing changes to create a culture where employees feel valued, engaged, and empowered to succeed.

Conduct a Culture Assessment:
Start by conducting a comprehensive assessment of your organization's culture. This may involve gathering feedback from employees through surveys, focus groups, and one-on-one interviews. Ask questions about values, behaviors, communication, leadership, and overall satisfaction to gain insight into the strengths and weaknesses of your culture.

Define Core Values and Behaviors:
Define clear and meaningful core values that reflect the identity, mission, and aspirations of your organization. Translate these values into actionable behaviors that guide decision-making, interactions, and behaviors at all levels of the organization. Ensure alignment between stated values and actual practices to create a culture of integrity, respect, and accountability.

Promote Open Communication:
Foster open communication channels where employees feel comfortable sharing feedback, ideas, and concerns. Encourage transparency and honesty in all communications, from leadership messages to team meetings. Actively listen to employee feedback and take action to address issues and implement changes based on their input.

Empower Employees:
Empower employees by providing opportunities for autonomy, decision-making, and professional development. Encourage employees to take ownership of their work, pursue learning opportunities, and contribute their unique talents and perspectives to the organization. Recognize and reward employees for their contributions and achievements to reinforce a culture of empowerment and appreciation.

Prioritize Diversity, Equity, and Inclusion (DEI):
Prioritize diversity, equity, and inclusion (DEI) initiatives to create a culture where all individuals feel valued, respected, and empowered to succeed. Implement programs and policies to promote diversity, address biases, and create opportunities for underrepresented groups. Foster a culture of belonging and allyship where employees feel supported and included regardless of their background or identity.

Support Well-being and Work-Life Balance:
Support employee well-being and promote work-life balance through policies and programs that prioritize physical, mental, and emotional health. Offer flexible work arrangements, wellness programs, and resources for stress management and self-care. Create a culture where employees feel encouraged to prioritize their well-being and maintain a healthy balance between work and personal life.

Lead by Example:
Leadership sets the tone for organizational culture. Lead by example by embodying the values and behaviors you wish to see in your organization. Demonstrate integrity, transparency, and humility in your actions and decisions. Listen to employee feedback, communicate openly, and show appreciation for their contributions. By leading by example, you inspire trust, confidence, and engagement among employees.

Continuously Evaluate and Improve:

Culture is not static; it evolves over time. Continuously evaluate your organization's culture and identify areas for improvement. Solicit feedback from employees, track key metrics related to culture and engagement, and adjust strategies and initiatives based on insights and feedback. Create a culture of continuous improvement where employees feel empowered to contribute to positive change and growth. In conclusion, assessing and improving your business culture is essential for creating a workplace where employees feel valued, engaged, and empowered to succeed. By conducting a culture assessment, defining core values and behaviors, promoting open communication, empowering employees, prioritizing diversity and inclusion, supporting well-being and work-life balance, leading by example, and continuously evaluating and improving, you can create a culture that drives success, satisfaction, and sustainable growth.

Chapter 30: Tools and Methods for Assessing Organizational Culture

Assessing organizational culture is a complex but crucial process for understanding the values, beliefs, and behaviors that shape the workplace environment. In this chapter, we explore various tools and methods that organizations can use to assess their culture effectively.

Employee Surveys:
Employee surveys are a common and valuable tool for assessing organizational culture. These surveys can include questions about values, communication, leadership, teamwork, and satisfaction. Use Likert scales, open-ended questions, and demographic information to gather comprehensive feedback from employees. Analyze survey results to identify trends, strengths, and areas for improvement within the culture.

Focus Groups:
Focus groups provide an opportunity for in-depth discussions and insights into organizational culture. Select a diverse group of employees to participate in facilitated discussions about culture-related topics. Encourage participants to share their experiences, perceptions, and suggestions for enhancing the culture. Use qualitative analysis techniques to identify common themes and patterns emerging from focus group discussions.

Interviews:

Conducting one-on-one interviews with employees, leaders, and stakeholders can offer valuable insights into organizational culture. Use structured interview guides to explore topics such as values, communication, leadership, and engagement. Encourage interviewees to share their perspectives, anecdotes, and suggestions for improving the culture. Analyze interview transcripts to identify recurring themes and areas for action.

Cultural Assessments:

Cultural assessments are formal evaluations of organizational culture conducted by external consultants or specialists. These assessments often involve a combination of surveys, interviews, focus groups, and observations to gather data about culture-related factors. Consultants analyze the data and provide recommendations for strengthening the culture based on their findings. Cultural assessments can provide valuable insights and actionable recommendations for improving organizational culture.

Cultural Audits:

Cultural audits involve reviewing organizational policies, practices, and artifacts to assess alignment with desired cultural values and behaviors. Review documents such as mission statements, employee handbooks, performance evaluations, and recognition programs to assess their impact on culture. Conduct observations of workplace interactions, meetings, and events to evaluate cultural norms and behaviors in action. Identify discrepancies between stated values and actual practices and develop strategies to address them.

Organizational Network Analysis (ONA):

ONA is a data-driven method for assessing communication, collaboration, and influence patterns within the organization. Analyze email communications, collaboration tools, and social network data to map connections and relationships between employees. Identify key influencers, information brokers, and communication bottlenecks within the organization. Use ONA insights to understand how culture manifests in communication and collaboration dynamics and identify opportunities for improvement.

Culture Assessment Tools:

Several culture assessment tools and frameworks are available to help organizations diagnose and understand their culture. Examples include the Organizational Culture Assessment Instrument (OCAI), the Denison Organizational Culture Survey (DOCS), and the Barrett Values Centre Cultural Transformation Tools (CTT). These tools typically involve surveys or assessments that measure cultural dimensions such as values, behaviors, and leadership practices. Use these tools to benchmark your organization's culture against industry standards and identify areas for development.

Pulse Surveys:

Pulse surveys are short, frequent surveys designed to capture real-time feedback from employees on specific culture-related topics. Use pulse surveys to track employee sentiment, engagement, and satisfaction over time. Ask targeted questions about culture-related initiatives, events, or changes to assess their impact and effectiveness. Use pulse survey data to inform decision-making and prioritize areas for action within the organization.

In conclusion, assessing organizational culture requires a multifaceted approach that combines qualitative and quantitative methods to gather insights from employees, leaders, and stakeholders. By using tools and methods such as employee surveys, focus groups, interviews, cultural assessments, ONA, culture assessment tools, and pulse surveys, organizations can gain a comprehensive understanding of their culture and identify opportunities for improvement and growth.

Chapter 31: Identifying Areas for Improvement

Identifying areas for improvement within organizational culture is essential for driving positive change and fostering a workplace environment where employees can thrive. In this chapter, we explore strategies for identifying areas for improvement and prioritizing actions to enhance organizational culture effectively.

Analyze Feedback and Data:
Start by analyzing feedback and data gathered from employee surveys, focus groups, interviews, cultural assessments, and other assessment tools. Look for recurring themes, trends, and patterns in the feedback to identify areas of strength and areas for improvement within the culture. Pay attention to both quantitative data, such as survey scores, and qualitative insights from open-ended responses and discussions.

Assess Alignment with Core Values:
Evaluate how well organizational practices, policies, and behaviors align with core values and desired cultural norms. Identify areas where there may be discrepancies between stated values and actual practices. Assess the impact of organizational policies and practices on culture and employee experience. Look for opportunities to reinforce alignment with core values and address any areas of misalignment.

Review Key Culture Drivers:

Review key culture drivers such as leadership, communication, collaboration, recognition, and employee development. Assess the effectiveness of leadership behaviors and practices in promoting desired cultural outcomes. Evaluate communication channels and practices for clarity, transparency, and inclusiveness. Examine collaboration dynamics and team interactions to identify opportunities for improvement. Review recognition programs and practices to ensure they align with cultural values and promote positive behaviors.

Identify Pain Points and Challenges:

Identify pain points and challenges that may be hindering a positive culture within the organization. These may include issues such as lack of trust, poor communication, resistance to change, or low morale. Engage employees in discussions to understand their perspectives and experiences. Use root cause analysis techniques to identify underlying causes of cultural challenges and develop targeted strategies to address them.

Solicit Employee Input and Ideas:

Solicit input and ideas from employees on how to improve organizational culture. Encourage employees to share their feedback, suggestions, and innovative ideas for enhancing culture. Use mechanisms such as suggestion boxes, town hall meetings, or online platforms to gather input from employees at all levels of the organization. Empower employees to take ownership of culture improvement initiatives and participate in co-creating solutions.

Benchmark Against Best Practices:

Benchmark your organization's culture against industry best practices and peer organizations. Research case studies, success stories, and benchmarks from organizations known for their positive cultures. Identify strategies and practices that have been effective in driving cultural change and improvement in similar organizations. Adapt best practices to fit the unique context and needs of your organization.

Conduct Gap Analysis:

Conduct a gap analysis to identify discrepancies between current culture and desired culture. Compare current cultural attributes, behaviors, and practices with the ideal state defined by core values and organizational goals. Identify gaps and areas where improvements are needed to bridge the divide between current and desired culture. Prioritize areas for improvement based on the magnitude of the gaps and their impact on organizational objectives.

Seek External Perspectives:

Seek external perspectives from consultants, experts, or advisors with experience in culture change and improvement. Engage external partners to conduct assessments, provide insights, and offer recommendations for enhancing organizational culture. Leverage their expertise and outside perspective to identify blind spots, challenge assumptions, and generate fresh ideas for culture improvement.

In conclusion, identifying areas for improvement within organizational culture requires a systematic approach that involves analyzing feedback and data, assessing alignment with core values, reviewing key culture drivers, identifying pain points and challenges, soliciting employee input, benchmarking against best practices, conducting gap analysis, and seeking external perspectives. By taking a holistic and proactive approach to culture improvement, organizations can create a workplace environment where employees feel valued, engaged, and empowered to succeed.

Chapter 32: Implementing Changes and Measuring Impact

Implementing changes to improve organizational culture requires thoughtful planning, effective execution, and ongoing evaluation. In this chapter, we explore strategies for implementing culture changes and measuring their impact to ensure positive outcomes and sustained progress.

Develop a Clear Action Plan:
Start by developing a clear action plan outlining the changes needed to improve organizational culture. Define specific goals, objectives, and desired outcomes for culture improvement initiatives. Identify key stakeholders, resources, and timelines for implementation. Break down larger goals into actionable steps and assign responsibilities to individuals or teams accountable for driving change.

Communicate the Vision and Rationale:
Communicate the vision for culture change and the rationale behind it to employees at all levels of the organization. Clearly articulate the benefits of the proposed changes and how they align with organizational values, goals, and priorities. Use multiple communication channels such as town hall meetings, email updates, intranet portals, and team meetings to ensure widespread awareness and understanding of the change initiative.

Foster Leadership Support and Alignment:

Gain buy-in and support from organizational leaders and managers for culture change initiatives. Engage leaders as champions and role models for the desired cultural behaviors and practices. Provide leadership training and support to equip leaders with the skills and tools needed to effectively drive culture change within their teams. Ensure alignment between leadership behaviors, decisions, and the desired cultural outcomes.

Empower Employees and Foster Ownership:

Empower employees to take ownership of culture change initiatives and actively participate in the change process. Create opportunities for employees to contribute their ideas, feedback, and suggestions for improving culture. Encourage bottom-up initiatives and grassroots efforts to drive change from within the organization. Provide resources, support, and recognition for employees leading culture improvement efforts.

Implement Pilot Programs and Quick Wins:

Implement pilot programs and quick wins to demonstrate progress and generate momentum for culture change. Start with small-scale initiatives that can be implemented quickly and easily to show tangible results. Celebrate successes and share stories of positive impact to inspire confidence and enthusiasm for culture improvement efforts. Use pilot programs as learning opportunities to gather feedback and refine strategies for broader implementation.

Monitor Progress and Adjust Strategies:

Continuously monitor progress toward culture change goals and objectives. Track key metrics, such as employee engagement scores, turnover rates, and cultural alignment assessments, to measure the impact of change initiatives. Collect feedback from employees on their experiences with culture change efforts and use this input to adjust strategies and tactics as needed. Stay agile and flexible in responding to emerging challenges and opportunities.

Provide Ongoing Training and Support:

Provide ongoing training and support to employees and leaders to reinforce desired cultural behaviors and practices. Offer workshops, seminars, and coaching sessions focused on topics such as communication, teamwork, diversity, and inclusion. Provide resources and tools to help employees navigate cultural change and overcome resistance or barriers to change. Create a culture of continuous learning and development that supports ongoing culture improvement efforts.

Celebrate Successes and Recognize Progress:
Celebrate successes and recognize progress made toward culture change goals. Acknowledge and reward individuals and teams that contribute to culture improvement efforts. Hold regular checkpoints or milestones to review progress, share updates, and celebrate achievements. Use recognition programs, awards, and ceremonies to publicly acknowledge and appreciate the efforts of employees driving positive cultural change.

In conclusion, implementing changes to improve organizational culture requires a systematic approach that involves developing a clear action plan, communicating the vision and rationale, fostering leadership support and alignment, empowering employees, implementing pilot programs and quick wins, monitoring progress, adjusting strategies, providing ongoing training and support, and celebrating successes. By following these strategies and principles, organizations can effectively drive culture change and create a workplace environment where employees feel valued, engaged, and empowered to succeed.

Chapter 33: The Future of Business Culture

As we look ahead, the future of business culture holds both exciting opportunities and new challenges. In this chapter, we explore emerging trends and shifts that are shaping the future of organizational culture and how businesses can adapt to thrive in the evolving landscape.

Embracing Remote and Hybrid Work:
The COVID-19 pandemic has accelerated the adoption of remote and hybrid work models, transforming the way organizations operate and interact. In the future, businesses will need to embrace flexible work arrangements and leverage technology to facilitate collaboration, communication, and connection among remote and distributed teams. Cultivating a culture of trust, autonomy, and accountability will be essential for supporting remote work and maintaining a sense of belonging and connection among employees.

Prioritizing Employee Well-being and Mental Health:
The growing awareness of the importance of employee well-being and mental health is reshaping organizational priorities and practices. In the future, businesses will need to prioritize initiatives that support employee well-being, resilience, and work-life balance. This may involve offering mental health resources, flexible work arrangements, wellness programs, and initiatives to promote a culture of care and support. By prioritizing employee well-being, organizations can enhance productivity, engagement, and retention in the long term.

Advancing Diversity, Equity, and Inclusion (DEI) Efforts:

The push for greater diversity, equity, and inclusion in the workplace is driving organizations to reexamine their culture and practices. In the future, businesses will need to advance DEI efforts by implementing inclusive policies, fostering a culture of belonging, and addressing systemic barriers to diversity and equity. This may involve initiatives such as unconscious bias training, diverse hiring practices, inclusive leadership development, and creating safe spaces for dialogue and allyship. By prioritizing DEI, organizations can unlock the full potential of their diverse workforce and drive innovation and growth.

Navigating Technological Advancements and Automation: Rapid technological advancements and automation are reshaping the nature of work and the skills required for success. In the future, businesses will need to navigate the impact of automation on job roles, workflows, and employee skills. This may involve upskilling and reskilling initiatives to prepare employees for the future of work, fostering a culture of continuous learning and adaptation, and embracing technology as an enabler of innovation and efficiency. By leveraging technology strategically, organizations can empower employees to thrive in an increasingly digital and automated world.

Cultivating a Culture of Adaptability and Resilience:
The pace of change and uncertainty in the business environment requires organizations to cultivate a culture of adaptability and resilience. In the future, businesses will need to embrace change as a constant and empower employees to navigate ambiguity, learn from failure, and innovate in response to evolving challenges and opportunities. This may involve fostering a growth mindset culture, promoting agility and flexibility in decision-making and operations, and creating structures and processes that enable rapid experimentation and iteration. By cultivating a culture of adaptability and resilience, organizations can thrive in an increasingly dynamic and unpredictable world.

Reimagining Leadership and Organizational Structures:
The future of business culture will require reimagining traditional notions of leadership and organizational structures. In the future, businesses will need to embrace distributed leadership models, flatten hierarchies, and empower employees at all levels to lead and influence change. This may involve fostering a culture of empowerment, trust, and collaboration, where leadership is distributed based on expertise, influence, and impact rather than formal authority. By reimagining leadership and organizational structures, organizations can unlock the full potential of their talent and adapt more effectively to complex and rapidly changing environments.

In conclusion, the future of business culture will be shaped by emerging trends such as remote and hybrid work, prioritizing employee well-being and mental health, advancing diversity, equity, and inclusion efforts, navigating technological advancements and automation, cultivating a culture of adaptability and resilience, and reimagining leadership and organizational structures. By embracing these trends and proactively adapting to change, businesses can create cultures that empower employees, drive innovation, and foster sustainable success in the years to come.

Chapter 34: Trends Shaping the Future of Work and Culture

As we step into the future, the intersection of work and culture is undergoing significant transformation driven by technological advancements, societal shifts, and evolving employee expectations. In this chapter, we delve into key trends that are shaping the future of work and organizational culture.

Remote and Hybrid Work:
The COVID-19 pandemic has accelerated the adoption of remote and hybrid work models, ushering in a new era of flexibility and decentralization. Organizations are embracing remote work as a long-term strategy, enabling employees to work from anywhere while maintaining productivity and collaboration through digital tools and platforms. The trend towards remote and hybrid work is reshaping organizational culture, emphasizing trust, autonomy, and results-oriented performance management.

Digital Transformation:
Digital transformation is revolutionizing the way businesses operate, interact, and deliver value. Emerging technologies such as artificial intelligence, automation, and data analytics are driving efficiency, innovation, and agility across industries. Organizations are leveraging technology to streamline processes, enhance customer experiences, and empower employees to work smarter and more collaboratively. Digital transformation is reshaping organizational culture by promoting agility, adaptability, and a culture of experimentation and learning.

Focus on Employee Well-being:

There is a growing recognition of the importance of employee well-being and mental health in the workplace. Organizations are prioritizing initiatives that support employee well-being, resilience, and work-life balance. From flexible work arrangements and wellness programs to mental health resources and supportive leadership practices, businesses are fostering cultures of care and compassion that promote employee engagement, productivity, and retention.

Diversity, Equity, and Inclusion (DEI):

The call for greater diversity, equity, and inclusion in the workplace is driving organizations to rethink their cultures and practices. Businesses are prioritizing DEI initiatives to create more inclusive and equitable workplaces where all individuals feel valued, respected, and empowered to succeed. From diverse hiring practices and inclusive leadership development to bias training and inclusive policies, organizations are fostering cultures of belonging and allyship that drive innovation, creativity, and performance.

Flexible Work Arrangements:

Flexibility in work arrangements is becoming increasingly important as employees seek greater autonomy and control over their schedules. Organizations are offering flexible work options such as flextime, compressed workweeks, and remote work to accommodate diverse employee needs and preferences. By providing flexibility, businesses are enhancing employee satisfaction, engagement, and retention while promoting a culture of trust, empowerment, and work-life balance.

Lifelong Learning and Skills Development:

The rapid pace of technological change and disruption is driving a growing demand for lifelong learning and skills development. Organizations are investing in employee training and development initiatives to upskill and reskill their workforce for the jobs of the future. From online learning platforms and microlearning opportunities to mentorship programs and skills-based hiring practices, businesses are fostering cultures of continuous learning and growth that enable employees to adapt and thrive in dynamic and evolving environments.

Remote Collaboration and Communication:

The shift towards remote work has elevated the importance of effective collaboration and communication in virtual environments. Organizations are leveraging digital collaboration tools and platforms to facilitate seamless communication, knowledge sharing, and teamwork across distributed teams. By embracing remote collaboration, businesses are fostering cultures of transparency, collaboration, and innovation that transcend geographical boundaries and enable employees to work together effectively regardless of location.

Agile and Adaptive Leadership:

The future of work demands agile and adaptive leadership that can navigate uncertainty, complexity, and change with resilience and vision. Leaders are embracing servant leadership principles, empathy, and humility to inspire and empower their teams. By fostering cultures of trust, transparency, and psychological safety, leaders are creating environments where employees feel empowered to take risks, experiment, and innovate in pursuit of shared goals and objectives.

In conclusion, the future of work and organizational culture is being shaped by trends such as remote and hybrid work, digital transformation, focus on employee well-being, diversity, equity, and inclusion, flexible work arrangements, lifelong learning and skills development, remote collaboration and communication, and agile and adaptive leadership. By embracing these trends and proactively adapting to change, businesses can create cultures that empower employees, drive innovation, and foster sustainable success in the years to come.

Chapter 35: Adapting to Technological Advancements

Technological advancements are reshaping the way we work, communicate, and interact. In this chapter, we explore how organizations can adapt to technological advancements to enhance productivity, collaboration, and innovation while fostering a positive organizational culture.

Embrace Digital Tools and Platforms:
In today's digital age, organizations must embrace a wide range of digital tools and platforms to streamline processes, enhance communication, and facilitate collaboration. From project management software and communication platforms to virtual meeting tools and cloud-based storage solutions, digital tools enable employees to work more efficiently and effectively, regardless of location. By providing employees with access to the latest digital technologies, organizations can empower them to work smarter and more collaboratively while promoting a culture of innovation and agility.

Invest in Employee Training and Development:
Technological advancements require employees to continuously update their skills and knowledge to stay relevant in their roles. Organizations must invest in employee training and development programs to upskill and reskill their workforce for the digital age. From technical skills training to digital literacy programs, organizations can equip employees with the tools and knowledge they need to leverage technology effectively in their roles. By investing in employee development, organizations not only enhance productivity and performance but also foster a culture of continuous learning and growth.

Foster a Culture of Experimentation and Innovation:
Technology provides organizations with opportunities to innovate and experiment in new ways. Leaders should encourage employees to explore new technologies, experiment with different tools and approaches, and embrace a culture of innovation and experimentation. By creating an environment where failure is seen as a learning opportunity rather than a setback, organizations can foster creativity, curiosity, and a willingness to take risks. By fostering a culture of experimentation and innovation, organizations can stay ahead of the curve and drive meaningful change in the digital age.

Promote Collaboration Across Teams and Departments:
Technology enables seamless collaboration and communication across teams and departments, regardless of geographical location. Organizations should leverage digital collaboration tools and platforms to break down silos, facilitate cross-functional collaboration, and promote knowledge sharing and idea exchange. By creating opportunities for employees to collaborate on projects, share insights, and learn from one another, organizations can foster a culture of teamwork, trust, and collaboration that drives innovation and success.

Prioritize Data Security and Privacy:
With the increasing reliance on technology comes the need for robust data security and privacy measures. Organizations must prioritize data security and privacy to protect sensitive information and safeguard against cyber threats. This involves implementing secure protocols, encryption techniques, and access controls to protect data at all stages of the digital workflow. By prioritizing data security and privacy, organizations can build trust with employees, customers, and partners while minimizing the risk of data breaches and cyber attacks.

Adapt Leadership Styles and Practices:

Technological advancements require leaders to adapt their leadership styles and practices to effectively lead in the digital age. Leaders should embrace a servant leadership mindset, empower employees to leverage technology to achieve their goals, and lead by example in embracing digital tools and platforms. By fostering a culture of transparency, collaboration, and adaptability, leaders can inspire trust and confidence among employees and drive meaningful change in the organization.

In conclusion, adapting to technological advancements requires organizations to embrace digital tools and platforms, invest in employee training and development, foster a culture of experimentation and innovation, promote collaboration across teams and departments, prioritize data security and privacy, and adapt leadership styles and practices. By embracing technology and leveraging it effectively, organizations can enhance productivity, collaboration, and innovation while fostering a positive organizational culture that empowers employees to succeed in the digital age.

Chapter 36: Anticipating and Managing Change

Change is inevitable in today's dynamic and fast-paced business environment. In this chapter, we explore strategies for anticipating and managing change effectively to foster a culture of adaptability, resilience, and continuous improvement within organizations.

Develop a Change-Ready Culture:
Cultivate a culture that embraces change as a natural and necessary part of growth and evolution. Encourage employees to adopt a growth mindset, where they view challenges as opportunities for learning and development. Foster open communication and transparency to keep employees informed about changes and involve them in the decision-making process. By creating a change-ready culture, organizations can empower employees to navigate uncertainty and embrace change with confidence.
Anticipate Future Trends and Challenges:
Stay ahead of the curve by anticipating future trends and challenges that may impact the organization. Conduct regular environmental scans to identify emerging technologies, market trends, regulatory changes, and competitive threats. Engage with industry experts, thought leaders, and stakeholders to gain insights into potential disruptors and opportunities. By staying informed and proactive, organizations can position themselves to adapt and thrive in the face of change.
Communicate Effectively:

Effective communication is essential for managing change successfully. Clearly articulate the rationale behind the change, the expected outcomes, and the role of employees in the process. Provide regular updates and opportunities for employees to ask questions, share feedback, and express concerns. Tailor communication messages to different audiences and channels to ensure information is delivered in a timely and accessible manner. By fostering open and transparent communication, organizations can build trust and alignment throughout the change process.

Empower Employees to Drive Change:

Empower employees to take ownership of change initiatives and drive meaningful progress within their teams and departments. Provide opportunities for employees to contribute their ideas, insights, and expertise to the change process. Encourage innovation and experimentation by creating a safe space for employees to test new ideas and approaches. Recognize and reward employees for their contributions to change efforts and celebrate milestones and achievements along the way. By empowering employees to drive change, organizations can harness the collective intelligence and creativity of their workforce to drive meaningful and sustainable change.

Provide Support and Resources:

Change can be challenging, and employees may require support and resources to navigate the process effectively. Offer training, coaching, and development opportunities to help employees build the skills and capabilities needed to adapt to change. Provide access to tools, resources, and support networks to help employees manage stress, build resilience, and maintain well-being during times of change. By investing in employee support and resources, organizations can minimize resistance to change and maximize engagement and productivity.

Monitor Progress and Adjust Strategies:

Monitor progress towards change goals and objectives and regularly assess the effectiveness of change strategies and initiatives. Collect feedback from employees, stakeholders, and customers to gauge perceptions and identify areas for improvement. Use data and metrics to track key performance indicators and measure the impact of change on organizational outcomes. Be willing to adjust strategies and tactics based on feedback and insights to ensure change efforts stay on track and deliver desired results.

Celebrate Successes and Learn from Failures:

Celebrate successes and milestones achieved throughout the change process to acknowledge the hard work and dedication of employees. Recognize individuals and teams for their contributions and achievements in driving change. At the same time, embrace failure as an opportunity for learning and growth. Encourage a culture of experimentation and risk-taking, where employees feel empowered to try new things and learn from both successes and setbacks. By celebrating successes and learning from failures, organizations can foster a culture of resilience and continuous improvement that drives ongoing success.

In conclusion, anticipating and managing change effectively requires organizations to cultivate a change-ready culture, anticipate future trends and challenges, communicate effectively, empower employees to drive change, provide support and resources, monitor progress and adjust strategies, and celebrate successes and learn from failures. By embracing change as an opportunity for growth and innovation, organizations can adapt and thrive in an ever-evolving business landscape.

Chapter 37: Recap of Key Points

Throughout this book, we've explored the importance of business culture and how it influences organizational success, employee engagement, and overall performance. Let's recap some of the key points discussed:

Understanding Business Culture:
Business culture encompasses the values, beliefs, behaviors, and norms that define how an organization operates and interacts with its employees, customers, and stakeholders. It shapes the workplace environment, employee experiences, and organizational outcomes.

Impact of Business Culture:
Business culture plays a significant role in driving organizational success, fostering employee satisfaction and retention, and shaping customer perceptions. A strong and positive culture can enhance collaboration, innovation, and performance, while a negative or toxic culture can lead to disengagement, turnover, and underperformance.

Elements of Business Culture:
Business culture is comprised of various elements, including core values, communication styles, organizational structure, work environment, rituals, and traditions. These elements collectively shape the identity and character of an organization and influence how employees interact and behave.

Building a Positive Business Culture:
Creating a positive business culture requires deliberate effort and commitment from organizational leaders and employees. It involves defining core values, fostering open communication, promoting collaboration and teamwork, and prioritizing employee well-being and development.

Managing Cultural Differences:

In an increasingly globalized world, organizations must navigate cultural differences and diversity to foster inclusive and equitable workplaces. This involves understanding and respecting cultural norms, promoting cultural sensitivity and awareness, and embracing diversity as a source of strength and innovation.

Adapting to Change and Technological Advancements: Organizations must be agile and adaptable to thrive in a rapidly changing business environment. This requires embracing technological advancements, anticipating future trends and challenges, and effectively managing change to foster a culture of resilience, innovation, and continuous improvement.

Empowering Employees:

Empowering employees to take ownership of their work, contribute their ideas, and drive change is essential for building a positive business culture. Organizations should provide opportunities for growth, recognize and reward contributions, and create a supportive and inclusive environment where employees feel valued and empowered to succeed.

In conclusion, business culture is a fundamental aspect of organizational success and employee well-being. By prioritizing culture, embracing diversity, fostering collaboration, and adapting to change, organizations can create environments where employees thrive, innovation flourishes, and long-term success is achieved.

Chapter 38: Final Thoughts on the Importance of Business Culture

As we conclude our exploration of the importance of business culture, it's essential to reflect on the profound impact that culture has on organizations, employees, and stakeholders. Business culture is more than just a set of values or practices; it's the heartbeat of an organization, shaping its identity, character, and destiny. Here are some final thoughts on why business culture matters:

Culture Drives Organizational Success:
A strong and positive culture is a powerful driver of organizational success. It influences employee engagement, motivation, and productivity, leading to higher levels of performance and innovation. Organizations with a strong culture are better equipped to attract and retain top talent, build strong relationships with customers and stakeholders, and adapt to changing market dynamics with agility and resilience.

Culture Shapes Employee Experience:
Business culture significantly impacts the employee experience, from recruitment and onboarding to daily interactions and career development. A positive culture promotes a sense of belonging, purpose, and fulfillment among employees, leading to higher job satisfaction, morale, and loyalty. Employees who feel valued, supported, and empowered by their organization are more likely to be motivated, engaged, and committed to achieving shared goals and objectives.

Culture Defines Organizational Identity:
Business culture defines the identity and character of an organization, shaping its reputation, brand, and competitive advantage. It reflects the collective values, beliefs, and behaviors of employees and leaders, influencing how the organization is perceived by internal and external stakeholders. A strong and distinctive culture can differentiate an organization in the marketplace, attracting customers, investors, and partners who align with its values and vision.

Culture Guides Decision-Making and Behavior:
Culture serves as a guidepost for decision-making and behavior within an organization. It sets the tone for how employees interact with one another, make decisions, and solve problems. A positive culture promotes ethical behavior, transparency, and accountability, fostering trust and credibility among employees and stakeholders. Leaders who embody the organization's culture inspire others to uphold its values and principles in their day-to-day actions and interactions.

Culture Fuels Innovation and Adaptability:
Business culture is a catalyst for innovation and adaptability, enabling organizations to thrive in an ever-changing business landscape. A culture that encourages creativity, risk-taking, and continuous learning empowers employees to challenge the status quo, experiment with new ideas, and embrace change with confidence. Organizations with a culture of innovation are better equipped to anticipate market trends, capitalize on emerging opportunities, and stay ahead of competitors in today's dynamic and competitive marketplace.

In essence, business culture is the soul of an organization, guiding its purpose, behavior, and impact on the world. By prioritizing culture, investing in its development, and nurturing it over time, organizations can create environments where employees feel inspired, valued, and empowered to achieve their full potential. As we move forward, let us remember that building a positive culture is not just a strategy for success; it's a commitment to creating a better, more inclusive, and sustainable future for all.

Conclusion: Call to Action: Building a Culture of Success

As we reach the end of our journey exploring the importance of business culture, it's time to turn our insights into action. Building a culture of success requires a collective effort from leaders, employees, and stakeholders at all levels of the organization. Here's a call to action for building a culture that fosters success and sustainability:

Commit to Values-Driven Leadership:
Leaders must lead by example and demonstrate a steadfast commitment to the organization's core values and principles. They should embody the desired cultural traits and behaviors, inspire others to do the same, and hold themselves and others accountable for upholding the organization's values in all actions and decisions.

Empower Employees to Thrive:
Empower employees to take ownership of their work, contribute their ideas, and drive positive change within the organization. Provide opportunities for growth, learning, and development, and create a supportive environment where employees feel valued, respected, and empowered to succeed.

Foster Open Communication and Collaboration:
Cultivate a culture of open communication, transparency, and collaboration where employees feel comfortable sharing ideas, providing feedback, and collaborating across teams and departments. Create channels and platforms for dialogue, encourage constructive debate, and foster a culture of inclusivity and belonging where diverse perspectives are valued and respected.

Prioritize Employee Well-being and Work-Life Balance:

Prioritize employee well-being and work-life balance by offering flexible work arrangements, wellness programs, and initiatives to support physical, mental, and emotional health. Recognize the importance of work-life balance in fostering employee engagement, productivity, and retention, and create policies and practices that promote a healthy and supportive workplace culture.

Embrace Diversity, Equity, and Inclusion:

Embrace diversity, equity, and inclusion as fundamental pillars of organizational culture. Create a culture that celebrates diversity, fosters inclusion, and promotes equity and fairness for all employees. Implement policies and practices that eliminate bias, address systemic barriers to diversity and inclusion, and create a culture of belonging where every individual feels valued, respected, and empowered to contribute their unique talents and perspectives.

Embrace Change and Adaptability:

Embrace change as a natural and necessary part of growth and evolution. Encourage a culture of adaptability, resilience, and continuous improvement where employees are empowered to embrace change, learn from failure, and innovate in response to evolving challenges and opportunities. Provide support, resources, and training to help employees navigate change effectively and thrive in a rapidly changing business landscape.

Measure and Evaluate Culture:

Measure and evaluate the effectiveness of organizational culture regularly to ensure alignment with strategic goals and objectives. Collect feedback from employees, customers, and stakeholders to gauge perceptions of culture and identify areas for improvement. Use data and metrics to track key performance indicators related to culture, such as employee engagement, retention, and satisfaction, and adjust strategies and initiatives accordingly.

In conclusion, building a culture of success requires intentional effort, commitment, and collaboration from all members of the organization. By prioritizing values-driven leadership, empowering employees, fostering open communication and collaboration, prioritizing employee well-being and work-life balance, embracing diversity, equity, and inclusion, embracing change and adaptability, and measuring and evaluating culture, organizations can create environments where employees thrive, innovation flourishes, and long-term success is achieved. Let us take action today to build cultures that inspire, empower, and drive meaningful impact in the world.

Appendix: Resources for Further Learning

For those eager to delve deeper into the world of business culture and organizational development, here are some valuable resources to explore:

Books:
"The Culture Code: The Secrets of Highly Successful Groups" by Daniel Coyle
"Drive: The Surprising Truth About What Motivates Us" by Daniel H. Pink
"Leaders Eat Last: Why Some Teams Pull Together and Others Don't" by Simon Sinek
"Dare to Lead: Brave Work. Tough Conversations. Whole Hearts." by Brené Brown
"The Fifth Discipline: The Art & Practice of The Learning Organization" by Peter M. Senge
Online Courses:
Coursera: Explore courses on organizational culture, leadership, and change management from top universities and institutions.
LinkedIn Learning: Access a wide range of courses on topics such as employee engagement, diversity and inclusion, and building high-performing teams.
Udemy: Discover courses on leadership development, communication skills, and organizational psychology to enhance your understanding of business culture.
Podcasts:
"Culture Happens" by Human Synergistics: A podcast exploring the impact of culture on organizations and strategies for creating positive cultural change.

"WorkLife with Adam Grant" by TED: Adam Grant explores the world of work and organizational psychology, offering insights into building thriving workplaces.

"The Brené Brown Podcast": Brené Brown shares insights on leadership, vulnerability, and creating cultures of belonging and trust.

Research Papers and Articles:

Harvard Business Review: Access a wealth of research papers and articles on topics such as organizational culture, employee engagement, and leadership development.

McKinsey & Company Insights: Explore insights and perspectives on organizational culture, change management, and talent development from McKinsey & Company.

Professional Associations and Networks:

Society for Human Resource Management (SHRM): Join a community of HR professionals and access resources, events, and best practices on organizational culture and employee engagement.

Association for Talent Development (ATD): Connect with learning and development professionals and explore resources and tools for building high-performing teams and cultures of excellence.

These resources offer valuable insights, tools, and strategies for individuals and organizations committed to fostering positive cultures and driving meaningful change. Whether you're a leader, HR professional, or aspiring to make a difference in your organization, continuous learning and exploration of business culture are key to unlocking the full potential of individuals and teams.

Tools and Assessments for Analyzing Organizational Culture

Analyzing organizational culture requires robust tools and assessments to gain insights into the values, beliefs, and behaviors that shape the workplace environment. Here are some commonly used tools and assessments for analyzing organizational culture:

Organizational Culture Assessment Instrument (OCAI): Developed by Cameron and Quinn, the OCAI helps organizations assess their current and desired culture based on four culture types: Clan, Adhocracy, Market, and Hierarchy. It provides a framework for understanding the dominant cultural traits within an organization and identifying areas for alignment and improvement.

Denison Organizational Culture Survey (DOCS): The DOCS measures organizational culture across four key dimensions: Mission, Adaptability, Involvement, and Consistency. It assesses the strengths and weaknesses of an organization's culture and provides actionable insights for enhancing performance and effectiveness.

Competing Values Framework (CVF): The CVF, developed by Quinn and Rohrbaugh, identifies four competing values within organizations: Clan, Adhocracy, Market, and Hierarchy. It helps organizations understand their cultural orientation and how it impacts performance, innovation, and adaptability.

Cultural Values Assessment (CVA):

The CVA, developed by Barrett Values Centre, assesses the values and beliefs that underpin organizational culture. It measures individual and organizational values across seven levels of consciousness and provides insights into alignment, engagement, and performance.

Hofstede's Cultural Dimensions Theory:

Hofstede's theory identifies six cultural dimensions that influence behavior and values within organizations: Power Distance, Individualism vs. Collectivism, Masculinity vs. Femininity, Uncertainty Avoidance, Long-Term vs. Short-Term Orientation, and Indulgence vs. Restraint. It provides a framework for understanding cultural differences and similarities across different countries and organizations.

Organizational Network Analysis (ONA):

ONA examines the informal social networks and relationships within an organization to understand how communication, collaboration, and influence flow. It helps identify key influencers, communication bottlenecks, and opportunities for strengthening organizational culture and performance.

Employee Surveys and Feedback Mechanisms:

Employee surveys, focus groups, and feedback mechanisms are essential tools for gathering qualitative and quantitative data on organizational culture. They provide insights into employee perceptions, experiences, and sentiment, allowing organizations to identify areas for improvement and track progress over time.

Interviews and Observations:

Interviews with employees, leaders, and stakeholders, coupled with direct observations of workplace dynamics and interactions, offer valuable qualitative insights into organizational culture. They provide context and depth to quantitative data and help uncover underlying cultural norms, behaviors, and attitudes.

By leveraging these tools and assessments, organizations can gain a comprehensive understanding of their current culture, identify areas for improvement, and develop strategies for fostering a positive and high-performing workplace environment.

Books:

"The Culture Code: The Secrets of Highly Successful Groups" by Daniel Coyle - Explores the key components of successful organizational cultures and how they drive performance and collaboration.

"Corporate Culture and Performance" by John P. Kotter and James L. Heskett - Examines the relationship between corporate culture and organizational performance, offering insights into building and sustaining a positive culture.

"Culture's Consequences: Comparing Values, Behaviors, Institutions, and Organizations Across Nations" by Geert Hofstede - Provides a comprehensive analysis of cultural dimensions and their impact on organizations and societies globally.

"Diagnosing and Changing Organizational Culture: Based on the Competing Values Framework" by Kim S. Cameron and Robert E. Quinn - Offers practical guidance on assessing and transforming organizational culture using the Competing Values Framework.

"The Fifth Discipline: The Art & Practice of The Learning Organization" by Peter M. Senge - Explores the concept of the learning organization and how culture influences organizational effectiveness and adaptability.

Articles:

"How to Build a Culture of Originality" by Adam Grant - Harvard Business Review article that discusses strategies for fostering a culture of innovation and creativity within organizations.

"The Eight Archetypes of Organizational Culture" by Charles O'Reilly and Michael Tushman - Harvard Business Review article that identifies eight common archetypes of organizational culture and their implications for performance and change.

"Why Culture Is Key" by DeAnne Aguirre, Rutger von Post, and Cindy Levy - McKinsey Quarterly article that explores the importance of culture in driving organizational performance and competitive advantage.

"The Role of Culture in Digital Transformation" by Gerald C. Kane, Doug Palmer, Anh Nguyen Phillips, David Kiron, and Natasha Buckley - MIT Sloan Management Review article that examines the role of culture in successful digital transformations and how organizations can overcome cultural barriers.

"How to Create a Workplace Culture That Attracts and Retains Millennials" by Jeanne Meister - Forbes article that offers insights into building a workplace culture that resonates with millennial employees.

Websites:

Harvard Business Review (HBR) - HBR offers a wealth of articles, case studies, and resources on organizational culture, leadership, and management.

McKinsey & Company Insights - McKinsey provides insights and perspectives on organizational culture, change management, and leadership development.

Society for Human Resource Management (SHRM) - SHRM offers resources, research, and best practices on organizational culture, employee engagement, and talent management.

Barrett Values Centre - Barrett Values Centre offers tools and resources for assessing and transforming organizational culture based on values-driven principles.

Culture Amp - Culture Amp provides employee feedback and analytics platforms to help organizations measure and improve their culture, engagement, and performance.

www.ingramcontent.com/pod-product-compliance
Lightning Source LLC
Chambersburg PA
CBHW050108230526
45470CB00004B/1729